DICTIONARY *of* DINOSAURS

DICTIONARY *of* DINOSAURS

WIDE EYED EDITIONS

PUBLISHER'S NOTE
New information about dinosaurs is being discovered all the time. Dinosaurs often change name, or their dates change once more information is found out about them. This means it's a very exciting field to get into and learn about. You could even discover or name the next dinosaur one day!

INTRODUCTION

WELCOME TO THIS BOOK! IN THESE PAGES, YOU WILL FIND DINOSAURS THAT HAVE BEEN DISCOVERED AND VERIFIED BY A DINOSAUR EXPERT. READ ON TO LEARN MORE ABOUT THE PREHISTORIC WORLD...

WHAT ARE DINOSAURS?

Dinosaurs are a group of prehistoric reptiles that dominated the land for over 160 million years. During this time, they evolved into many different shapes and sizes, from the turkey-sized *Microraptor* to the fearsome giant *Spinosaurus*. They had bony skeletons and leathery skin, and were well-adapted to survive in a variety of habitats such as deserts, open plains, forests, and wetlands.

One of the reasons for the success of the dinosaurs is that they had straight legs, which were positioned directly underneath their bodies in an "erect" stance. This allowed them to move faster than reptiles that had a "sprawling" stance—like today's lizards and crocodiles.

DINOSAUR: *Aucasaurus*

ERECT STANCE

SPRAWLING STANCE

LIZARD: *Komodo Dragon*

WHEN DID DINOSAURS LIVE?

Dinosaurs lived between 230 and 66 million years ago, in a time known as the Mesozoic Era. This was many millions of years before the first modern humans, *Homo sapiens*, appeared. Most dinosaur species became extinct around 66 million years ago, but the descendants of one dinosaur group, the birds, are still with us today! Look at the timeline on pages 4–5 to find out more.

BIRD: *Secretary Bird*

WHAT KILLED OFF THE DINOSAURS?

The end of the Cretaceous Period saw one of the most dramatic extinctions that the Earth has ever seen. 66 million years ago, over a relatively short time, all the dinosaurs—except for birds—disappeared. Many other animals also died out, including flying pterosaurs, large marine reptiles, and other sea creatures, such as ammonites. Although the number of dinosaurs was already declining by this time, this suggests that a sudden catastrophic event sealed their fate. This event caused dramatic changes to the environment that would have happened more quickly than the dinosaurs could adapt to. The exact nature of this catastrophic event is still not clear. It could have been an asteroid impact, volcanic eruptions, or the effects of both, together with more gradual changes in the Earth's climate—all happening over millions of years. Whatever the causes, the huge extinction that ended the age of the dinosaurs left gaps in the ecosystem, which were then filled by mammals and birds.

HOW DO WE KNOW ABOUT DINOSAURS?

We know about the dinosaurs because of fossils. Fossils are animals or plants that died thousands of years ago, and have since turned to stone. "Body" fossils are the remains of an animal body. "Trace" fossils are remains that show animal activity, such as footprints or eggshells. All of them give us clues as to what the prehistoric world was like. Scientists known as paleontologists use special tools to dig up land and look for these fossils.

HOW DO FOSSILS FORM?

Fossils form when material falls into sand or mud. More layers of sand and mud build on top until the material dissolves. The sand or mud then hardens, leaving a hole, which preserves an impression of the original material. This is called a "mold fossil." Sometimes other material or minerals fill the hole and this is called a "cast fossil."

TRACE FOSSIL

BODY FOSSIL

Pisanosaurus

TIMELINE

DINOSAURS LIVED IN THE MESOZOIC ERA. SCIENTISTS DIVIDE THE MESOZOIC ERA INTO THREE PERIODS: THE TRIASSIC, JURASSIC, AND CRETACEOUS. DURING THIS TIME, THE LAND GRADUALLY SPLIT UP FROM ONE HUGE CONTINENT INTO SMALLER ONES. THE CHANGES IN THE WEATHER AND PLANT LIFE AFFECTED HOW DINOSAURS EVOLVED. LOOK AT THE TIMELINE TO SEE WHAT THE WORLD WAS LIKE THROUGH THE DIFFERENT TIME PERIODS.

TRIASSIC PERIOD (250–200 MILLION YEARS AGO)

During the Triassic Period, all the continents were part of a single land mass called Pangaea. This meant that there weren't many differences between the animals or plants found in different areas. The climate was relatively hot and dry, and much of the land was covered with large deserts. Unlike today, there were no polar ice caps. It was in this environment that the reptiles known as dinosaurs first evolved. Toward the end of the Triassic, a series of earthquakes and volcanic eruptions caused Pangaea to slowly begin to break into two. There was a mass extinction—but scientists are not sure why. Many large land animals were wiped out, but the dinosaurs survived, giving them the opportunity to evolve into a wide variety of forms and increase in number.

Giraffatitan

Triceratops

JURASSIC PERIOD
(200–145 MILLION YEARS AGO)

The single land mass, Pangaea, continued to split into two, creating Laurasia in the north and Gondwana in the south. Despite this separation, there were bridges between the two continents. Temperatures fell slightly, although it was still warmer than today. Rainfall increased as a result of the large seas appearing between the land masses. All these changes allowed plants such as ferns and horsetails to grow over wide areas. Elsewhere, there were forests of tall conifer trees such as sequoias and monkey puzzles. The plentiful plant supply allowed the huge plant-eating sauropods—such as *Apatosaurus*, *Diplodocus*, and *Brachiosaurus*—to evolve. The sauropods are the largest animals to have ever walked the Earth and their herds dominated the landscape by the end of the Jurassic.

CRETACEOUS PERIOD
(145–66 MILLION YEARS AGO)

During the Cretaceous Period, the land separated further into some of the continents we know today, although they were in different positions. This meant that dinosaurs evolved independently in different parts of the world, so they became more distinct from one another.

The first snakes evolved during this time, as well as the first flowering plants. A variety of insect groups appeared, including bees, which helped increase the spread of flowering plants. Mammals now included tree climbers, ground dwellers, and even predators of small dinosaurs. Then, 66 million years ago, came the mass extinction event—and the end of the Mesozoic Era.

HOW TO USE THIS BOOK

FACT FILE: This gives you statistics on its size, diet, when it lived, and where.

SCALE: The human model is 6 feet tall and shows you how big the dinosaurs were.

LATIN NAME: Each dinosaur has scientific name, a Latin name that is the same in all languages.

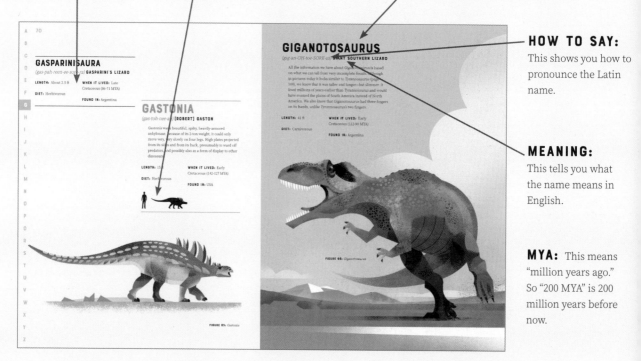

HOW TO SAY: This shows you how to pronounce the Latin name.

MEANING: This tells you what the name means in English.

MYA: This means "million years ago." So "200 MYA" is 200 million years before now.

Scientists group dinosaurs together based on how they would have looked or behaved. Here are the names of some dinosaur groups you might come across in this book:

THE ANKYLOSAURS: armored dinosaurs

THE CERATOPSIANS: dinosaurs with parrot-like beaks, bony frills, and horned faces

THE HADROSAURS: dinosaurs with broad, flat snouts and toothless beaks

THE PACHYCEPHALOSAURS: dinosaurs with thick, ridged skulls

EARLY SAUROPODS: long-necked dinosaurs with small heads that are thought to be ancestors to later sauropods

THE SAUROPODS: long-necked dinosaurs with small heads and long tails

THE STEGOSAURS: dinosaurs with hard bony plates on their backs

THE THEROPODS: meat-eating dinosaurs with short arms that walked on two legs

THE TITANOSAURS: the last-surviving (and largest) sauropods to walk the Earth

A - B

AARDONYX

(ar-don-ix) **EARTH CLAW**

We know about *Aardonyx* from two exciting fossil finds in South Africa, which show that it mainly walked on its hind two legs but was also able to drop and walk on all four legs. This means it could be the evolutionary link between the early dinosaur groups that came before it (plant-eating, long-necked dinosaurs that walked on two legs) and the huge sauropods that came after it (who walked on all four legs).

LENGTH: Over 26 ft

DIET: Herbivorous

WHEN IT LIVED: Early Jurassic (200–190 MYA)

FOUND IN: South Africa

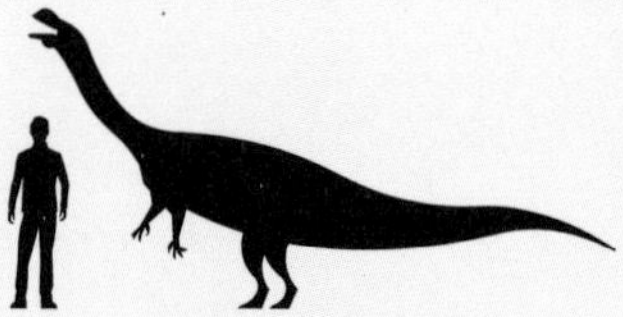

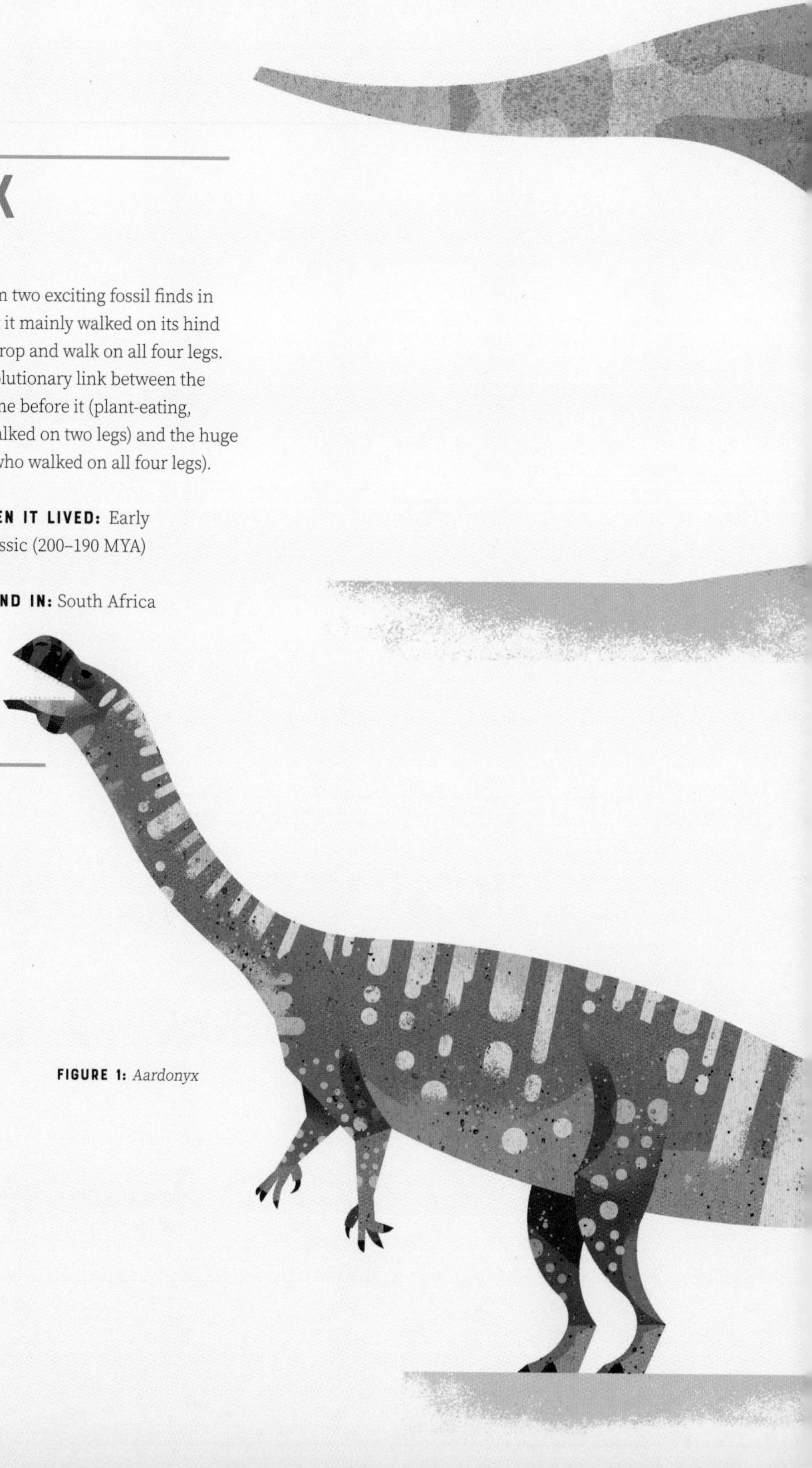

FIGURE 1: *Aardonyx*

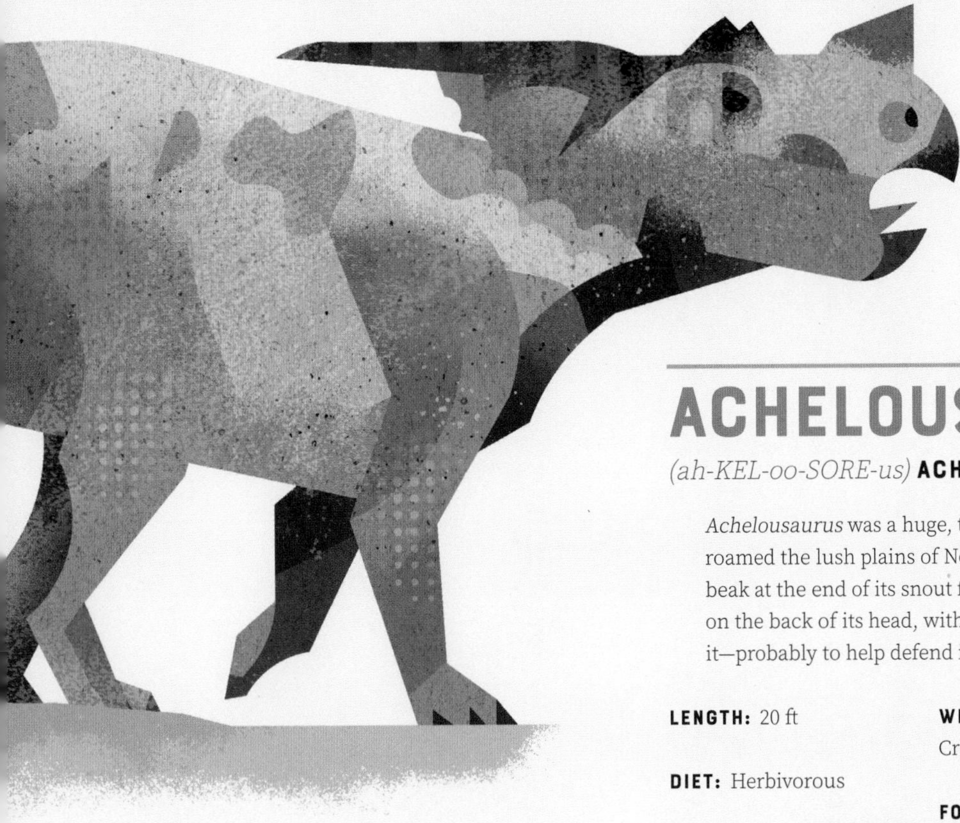

FIGURE 2: *Achelousaurus*

ACHELOUSAURUS

(ah-KEL-oo-SORE-us) **ACHELOUS' LIZARD**

Achelousaurus was a huge, tanklike herbivore that roamed the lush plains of North America. It had a sharp beak at the end of its snout for cropping leaves and a frill on the back of its head, with long spikes coming out of it—probably to help defend itself from predators.

LENGTH: 20 ft

DIET: Herbivorous

WHEN IT LIVED: Late Cretaceous (83-70 MYA)

FOUND IN: USA

ABELISAURUS

(ah-BELL-ee-sore-us) **ABEL'S LIZARD**

LENGTH: 30 ft

DIET: Carnivorous

WHEN IT LIVED: Late Cretaceous (74-70 MYA)

FOUND IN: Argentina

ACHILLOBATOR

(a-kil-oh-bah-tor) **ACHILLES HERO**

LENGTH: 16 ft

DIET: Carnivorous

WHEN IT LIVED: Late Cretaceous (99-84 MYA)

FOUND IN: Mongolia

ACROCANTHOSAURUS

(ah-kroh-kan-tho-SORE-us) **HIGH-SPINED LIZARD**

LENGTH: 40 ft

DIET: Carnivorous

WHEN IT LIVED: Early Cretaceous (115-105 MYA)

FOUND IN: Canada and USA

B
C
D
E
F
G
H
I
J
K
L
M
N
O
P
Q
R
S
T
U
V
W
X
Y
Z

AEGYPTOSAURUS

(ee-JIP-toe-SORE-us) **EGYPTIAN LIZARD**

LENGTH: 50 ft

WHEN IT LIVED: Late Cretaceous (98-93 MYA)

DIET: Herbivorous

FOUND IN: Egypt

FIGURE 3: *Afrovenator*

AFROVENATOR

(aff-ROW-ven-ah-tor) **AFRICAN HUNTER**

Afrovenator was bipedal (which means that it moved on two legs) and had three big claws on its hands. It was a large predator that probably hunted the sauropods of Africa, like *Jobaria*, using its sharp teeth to kill and devour its prey. It is believed to be a close relative of *Megalosaurus* (page 103), which lived during the Jurassic Period.

LENGTH: 30 ft

WHEN IT LIVED: Late Jurassic (167-157 MYA)

DIET: Carnivorous

FOUND IN: Niger

AGILISAURUS

(aj-i-li-sore-us) **AGILE LIZARD**

This agile and lightweight little dinosaur lived alongside the bigger dinosaurs of China, like *Huayangosaurus* (page 80), and probably ate the plants the bigger animals left behind. Its main defense against other dinosaurs was the speed at which it could run, which it would have used to keep out of the way of predators like *Gasosaurus* (page 69).

LENGTH: 5 ft

DIET: Herbivorous

WHEN IT LIVED: Late Jurassic (169-159 MYA)

FOUND IN: People's Republic of China

FIGURE 4: *Agilisaurus*

ALAMOSAURUS

(ah-la-mow-SORE-us) **ALAMO LIZARD**

LENGTH: 70 ft

DIET: Herbivorous

WHEN IT LIVED: Late Cretaceous (70-65 MYA)

FOUND IN: USA

ALBERTACERATOPS

(al-bert-a-serra-tops) **ALBERTA HORNED FACE**

This dinosaur surprised scientists when it was discovered, because unlike its close relatives, it had long brow horns similar to those of *Triceratops* (page 165). But unlike *Triceratops*, *Albertaceratops* did not have a large spike on its nose, but a banana-shaped bump. On top of its neck frill, in the center, it also had two small, curved spikes.

LENGTH: 20 ft

DIET: Herbivorous

WHEN IT LIVED: Late Cretaceous (80-75 MYA)

FOUND IN: Canada and USA

ALBERTOSAURUS

(al-BERT-oh-saw-russ) **ALBERTA LIZARD**

LENGTH: 30 ft

DIET: Carnivorous

WHEN IT LIVED: Late Cretaceous (76-74 MYA)

FOUND IN: Canada

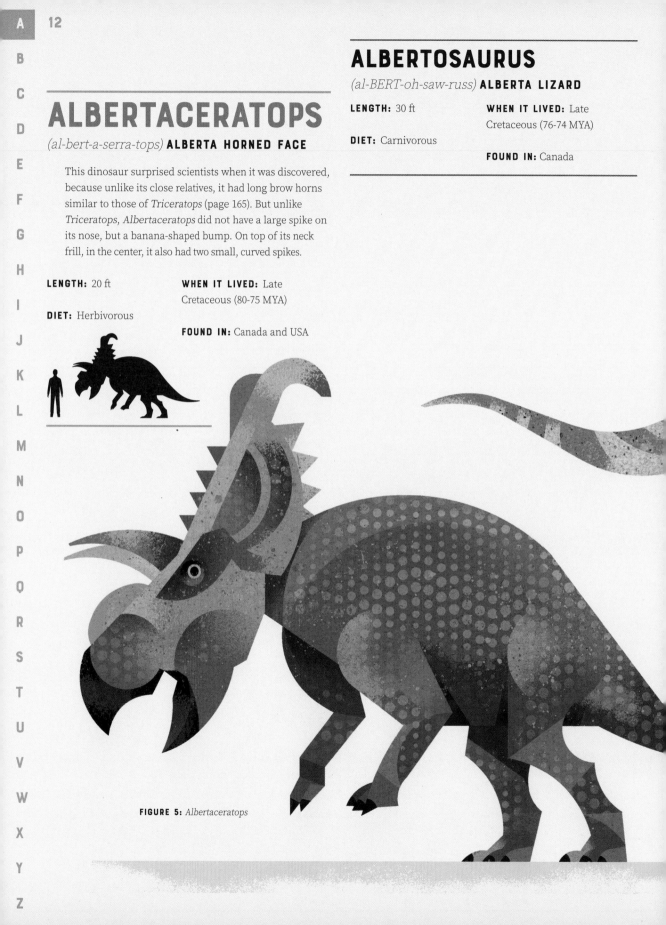

FIGURE 5: *Albertaceratops*

ALECTROSAURUS

(ah-LEK-tro-sore-us) **EAGLE LIZARD**

LENGTH: 16 ft

DIET: Carnivorous

WHEN IT LIVED: Late Cretaceous (90-70 MYA)

FOUND IN: People's Republic of China and Mongolia

FIGURE 6: *Alioramus*

ALIORAMUS

(al-ee-oh-ray-mus) **OTHER EVOLUTIONARY BRANCH**

The skull of this meat-eater shows small bumps near the nose. They were probably used for display, or possibly to help members of the same species recognize each other. *Alioramus* was a tyrannosaur, closely related to *Tyrannosaurus* (page 169), but it was much smaller—it would only have been about the height of a fully grown person.

LENGTH: 20 ft

DIET: Carnivorous

WHEN IT LIVED: Late Cretaceous (71-65 MYA)

FOUND IN: Mongolia

ALLOSAURUS

(AL-oh-saw-russ) **OTHER LIZARD**

In most parts of the world, *Allosaurus* would have been the most powerful and dangerous predator of its time, preying on *Stegosaurus* (page 153) and long-necked sauropods. Its teeth were an enormous 2–4 inches long and curved backward to prevent prey from escaping once it had clamped down with its jaws. *Allosaurus* would have lived a violent life, but it was tough enough to survive even the most painful wounds—like those from the spikes on the tail of *Stegosaurus*.

LENGTH: 40 ft

DIET: Carnivorous

WHEN IT LIVED: Late Jurassic (156-144 MYA)

FOUND IN: Portugal and USA

FIGURE 7: *Allosaurus*

ALVAREZSAURUS

(al-var-rez-SORE-us) **ALVAREZ'S LIZARD**

This bizarre-looking dinosaur belongs to the same family as modern birds. Like birds, scientists think it had a beak, which it may have used to eat insects, berries, roots, and leaves. It also had feathers, but it could not fly. Strangest of all, it had tiny arms and just one finger on each hand—possibly used to dig for food.

FIGURE 8: *Alvarezsaurus*

LENGTH: 6.5 ft

DIET: Carnivorous

WHEN IT LIVED:
Late Cretaceous
(89-85 MYA)

FOUND IN: Argentina

AMARGASAURUS

(A-MARG-oh-sore-us) **AMARGA LIZARD**

This magnificent sauropod stood out among all the other tree-browsing dinosaurs of its time. It had two rows of large spines protruding out of its neck and back. Scientists think that they may have supported two long sails of skin, which could have been used for display or signaling. It was probably hunted by predators like *Carnotaurus* (page 39).

LENGTH: 40 ft

DIET: Herbivorous

WHEN IT LIVED: Early
Cretaceous (132-127 MYA)

FOUND IN: Argentina

FIGURE 9: *Amargasaurus*

A
B
C
D
E
F
G
H
I
J
K
L
M
N
O
P
Q
R
S
T
U
V
W
X
Y
Z

AMMOSAURUS

(ah-moh-SORE-us) **SAND LIZARD**

This dinosaur was so similar to *Anchisaurus* (page 18) that some scientists actually think they are the same species. Both dinosaurs were small to medium-sized tree browsers, and both probably walked on two legs.

LENGTH: 16 ft

DIET: Herbivorous

WHEN IT LIVED: Early Jurassic (195-180 MYA)

FOUND IN: USA

FIGURE 10: *Ammosaurus*

FIGURE 11: *Ampelosaurus*

AMPELOSAURUS

(am-pel-oh-sore-us) **VINEYARD LIZARD**

Over 500 *Ampelosaurus* bones have been found so far, and from what we know, it was quite a large, long-necked herbivore. Its thick, heavy arm bones suggest it would have been strong and bulky, weighing over 40 tons. But this would have also made it very slow, and a good target for fast-running predators like *Megalosaurus* (page 103).

LENGTH: 50 ft

DIET: Herbivorous

WHEN IT LIVED: Late Cretaceous (71-65 MYA)

FOUND IN: France

ANATOTITAN

(an-at-oh-TIE-tan) **GIANT DUCK**

Anatotitan was a gigantic herbivore that could walk on two legs, but probably used four most of the time. It moved around in herds, cropping leaves and grasses with its big, flat beak. Some scientists think that *Anatotitan* is actually the same dinosaur as *Edmontosaurus* (page 59), because they looked similar and lived at the same time.

LENGTH: 30 ft

DIET: Herbivorous

WHEN IT LIVED: Late Cretaceous (70-65 MYA)

FOUND IN: USA

FIGURE 12: *Anatotitan*

AMYGDALODON

(am-ig-dal-oh-don) **ALMOND TOOTH**

LENGTH: 50 ft

DIET: Herbivorous

WHEN IT LIVED: Mid Jurassic (177-169 MYA)

FOUND IN: Argentina

ANCHICERATOPS

(an-key-SERRA-tops) **NEAR HORNED LIZARD**

LENGTH: 20 ft

DIET: Herbivorous

WHEN IT LIVED: Late Cretaceous (74-70 MYA)

FOUND IN: Canada

ANCHISAURUS

(ANK-ee-sore-us) **NEAR LIZARD**

Anchisaurus was an ancestor to the much larger, longer-necked tree-browsers that dominated most of North America during the later Jurassic Period. It almost certainly walked on two legs, and perhaps used its hands to grasp at vegetation.

LENGTH: 6.5 ft

DIET: Herbivorous

WHEN IT LIVED: Early Jurassic (200 MYA)

FOUND IN: USA

ANKYLOSAURUS

(an-KIE-loh-sore-us) **STIFF LIZARD**

Ankylosaurus was an ankylosaur (an armored dinosaur) with a wide, heavily armored skull and a large tail club. Its armor would have covered every part of its body, including its eyelids, and the club on its tail could be swung with serious force—threatening any dinosaur that got in its way.

LENGTH: 23 ft

DIET: Herbivorous

WHEN IT LIVED: Late Cretaceous (74-67 MYA)

FOUND IN: Canada and USA

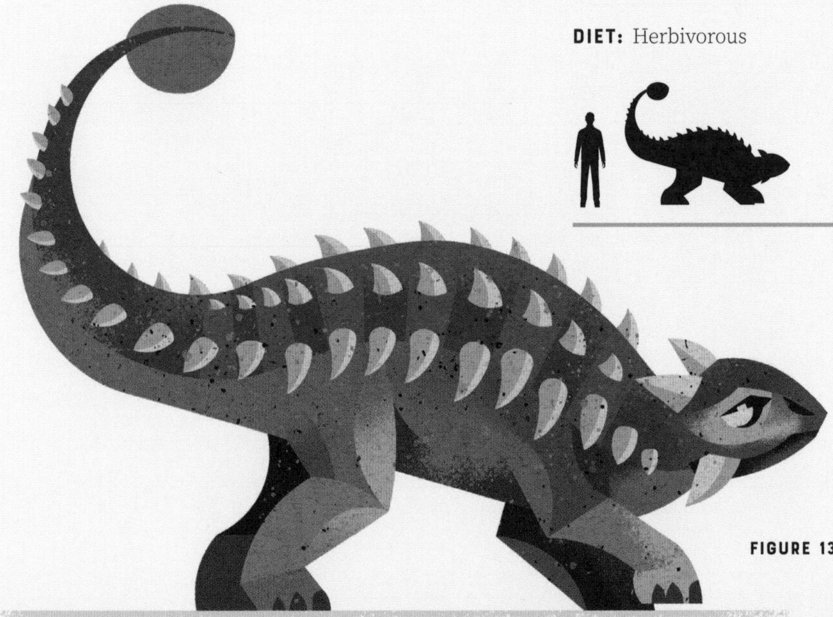

FIGURE 13: *Ankylosaurus*

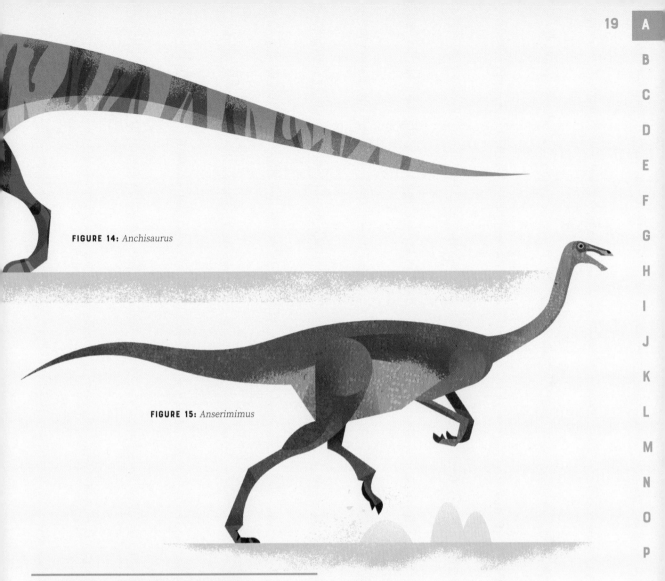

FIGURE 14: *Anchisaurus*

FIGURE 15: *Anserimimus*

ANSERIMIMUS

(ANN-ser-ih-mee-muss) **GOOSE MIMIC**

Anserimimus is so-named because it resembled living birds in many ways, including having a toothless beak at the end of its snout. This beak was probably used for breaking up plant material, but some scientists think *Anserimimus* may also have eaten meat—either from hunting or from scavenging dead animals.

LENGTH: 11 ft

DIET: Carnivorous

WHEN IT LIVED: Late Cretaceous (84-65 MYA)

FOUND IN: Mongolia

ANTARCTOPELTA

(ant-arc-toe-pel-ta) **ANTARCTIC SHIELD**

LENGTH: 13 ft

DIET: Herbivorous

WHEN IT LIVED: Late Cretaceous (99-94 MYA)

FOUND IN: Antarctica

B
C
D
E
F
G
H
I
J
K
L
M
N
O
P
Q
R
S
T
U
V
W
X
Y
Z

ANTARCTOSAURUS

(ant-ARK-toe-sore-us) **NON-NORTHERN LIZARD**

Despite its misleading name, *Antarctosaurus* hasn't been found on the continent of Antarctica, although some dinosaurs have been found there. The bones of this extremely large sauropod were actually found in South America—its name simply refers to the fact that it was from the very far south.

LENGTH: About 100 ft

DIET: Herbivorous

WHEN IT LIVED: Cretaceous (80 MYA)

FOUND IN: South America

APATOSAURUS

(ah-PAT-oh-sore-us) **DECEPTIVE LIZARD**

LENGTH: 70 ft

DIET: Herbivorous

WHEN IT LIVED: Late Jurassic (154-145 MYA)

FOUND IN: USA

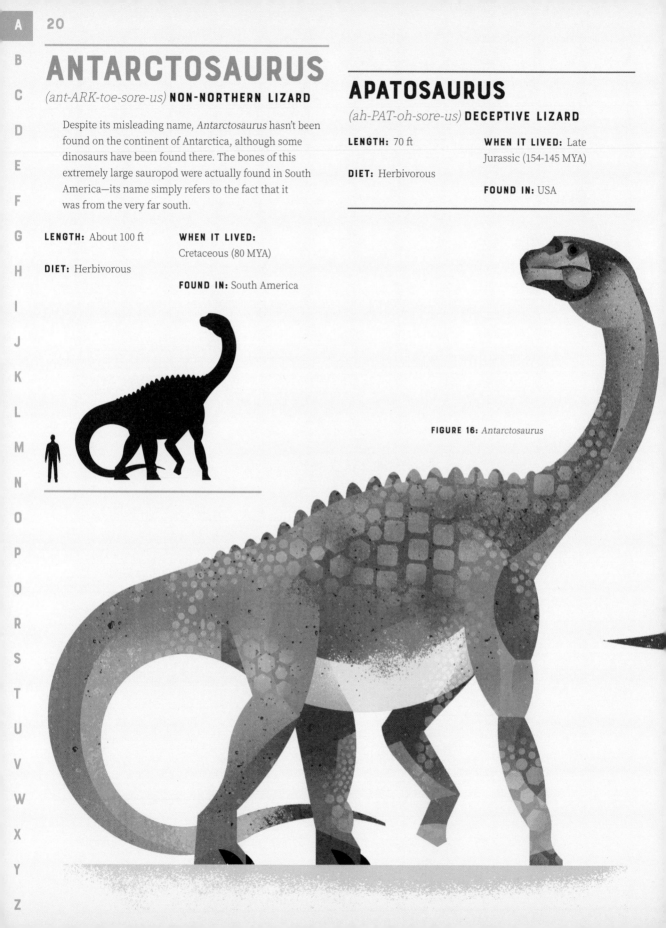

FIGURE 16: *Antarctosaurus*

B
C
D
E
F
G
H
I
J
K
L
M
N
O
P
Q
R
S
T
U
V
W
X
Y
Z

ARAGOSAURUS

(ahr-ah-go-sore-us) **ARAGÓN LIZARD**

LENGTH: 60 ft

WHEN IT LIVED: Early Cretaceous (132-121 MYA)

DIET: Herbivorous

FOUND IN: Spain

ARALOSAURUS

(ar-al-oh-sore-us) **ARAL LIZARD**

Aralosaurus was a beaked herbivore, and probably stood at the same height as a modern-day elephant. On its nose was a big lump of bone that formed a thick crest. Scientists believe this was too fragile for head-butting rivals, so it was probably for display.

LENGTH: 26 ft

WHEN IT LIVED: Late Cretaceous (94-84 MYA)

DIET: Herbivorous

FOUND IN: Kazakhstan

ARCHAEOCERATOPS

(ahr-kee-oh-serra-tops) **ANCIENT HORNED FACE**

LENGTH: 4 ft

WHEN IT LIVED: Early Cretaceous (121-99 MYA)

DIET: Herbivorous

FOUND IN: People's Republic of China

FIGURE 17: *Aralosaurus*

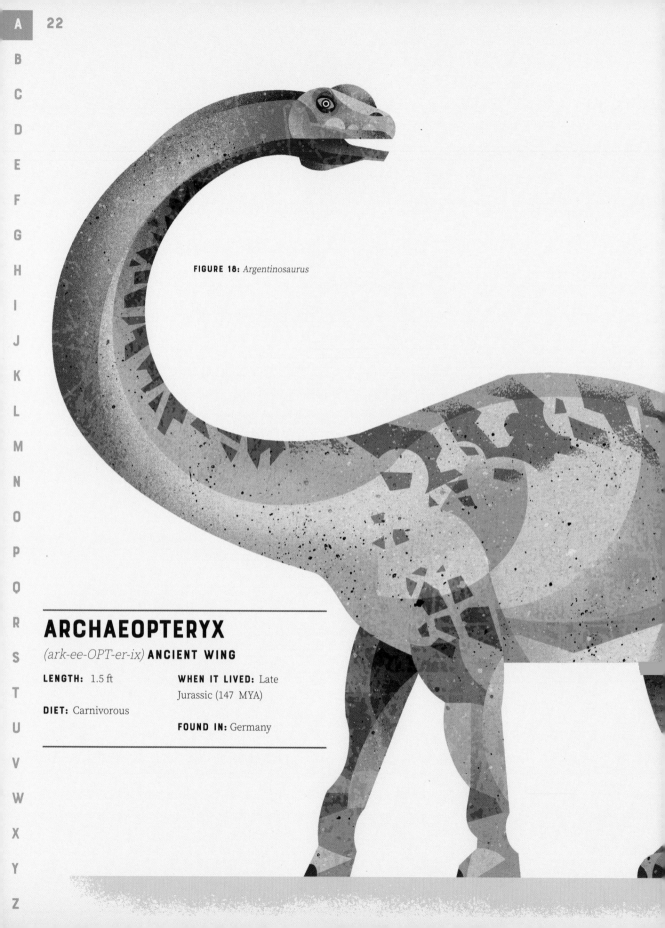

FIGURE 18: *Argentinosaurus*

ARCHAEOPTERYX
(ark-ee-OPT-er-ix) **ANCIENT WING**

LENGTH: 1.5 ft

DIET: Carnivorous

WHEN IT LIVED: Late Jurassic (147 MYA)

FOUND IN: Germany

ARGENTINOSAURUS

(AR-gent-eeno-sore-us) **ARGENTINA LIZARD**

The largest land animal ever found, *Argentinosaurus* did not stop growing during its lifetime. It probably used its long neck to sweep the ground or to reach high up in search of vegetation. It would have taken the hatchlings of *Argentinosaurus* 15 years to grow to adulthood, and in that time they would have been very vulnerable to predators, such as *Giganotosaurus* (page 71).

LENGTH: 115 ft

WHEN IT LIVED: Late Cretaceous (90 MYA)

DIET: Herbivorous

FOUND IN: Argentina

ARCHAEORNITHOMIMUS

(ark-ee-orn-ith-oh-mime-us) **ANCIENT BIRD MIMIC**

LENGTH: 11 ft

DIET: Carnivorous

WHEN IT LIVED: Late Cretaceous (95-70 MYA)

FOUND IN: People's Republic of China

ARRHINOCERATOPS

(ay-rine-oh-ker-ah-tops) **WITHOUT-NOSE-HORN FACE**

Everything we know about *Arrhinoceratops* is based on a single skull, as so little of this dinosaur has been found. However, we know that this ceratopsian (dinosaurs with parrot-like beaks, bony frills, and horned faces) lived just before its more famous cousin, *Triceratops*. Scientists believe that ceratopsians' head displays were used to tell each other apart, or to attract mates.

LENGTH: 20-26 ft

DIET: Herbivorous

WHEN IT LIVED: Late Cretaceous (72-67 MYA)

FOUND IN: Canada

ATLASCOPCOSAURUS

(atlass-KOP-KO-sore-us) **ATLAS COPCO LIZARD**

LENGTH: 10 ft

DIET: Herbivorous

WHEN IT LIVED: Early Cretaceous (121-97 MYA)

FOUND IN: Australia

FIGURE 19: *Arrhinoceratops*

FIGURE 20: *Aucasaurus*

AUCASAURUS

(aw-ka-sore-us) **AUCA LIZARD**

Aucasaurus was a powerfully built predator with a large
and strong skull. It must have had a powerful bite, too, as
its arms were very small and would not have been able to
hold on to prey by themselves. It probably hunted large
sauropod dinosaurs, but may also have eaten smaller
herbivores like *Gasparinisaura* (page 70).

LENGTH: 16 ft

DIET: Carnivorous

WHEN IT LIVED: Late
Cretaceous (84-71 MYA)

FOUND IN: Argentina

AUSTRALOVENATOR

(aw-strah-low-ven-ah-tor) **SOUTHERN HUNTER**

LENGTH: 20 ft

DIET: Carnivorous

WHEN IT LIVED: Late
Cretaceous (95-90 MYA)

FOUND IN: Australia

B
C
D
E
F
G
H
I
J
K
L
M
N
O
P
Q
R
S
T
U
V
W
X
Y
Z

AUSTROSAURUS

(aws-troh-sore-us) **SOUTH LIZARD**

Only fossils of fragmentary remains of *Austrosaurus* have been found so far—in Australia, as its name suggests. By comparing them to the fossils of other, similar dinosaurs, we can tell that it was quite a large sauropod. It would have walked slowly on all four legs to feed on the foliage of trees.

LENGTH: 50 ft

WHEN IT LIVED: Early Cretaceous (112-100 MYA)

DIET: Herbivorous

FOUND IN: Australia

AVACERATOPS

(ay-va-ker-ah-tops) **AVA'S HORNED FACE**

LENGTH: 7.5 ft

WHEN IT LIVED: Late Cretaceous (80-75 MYA)

DIET: Herbivorous

FOUND IN: USA

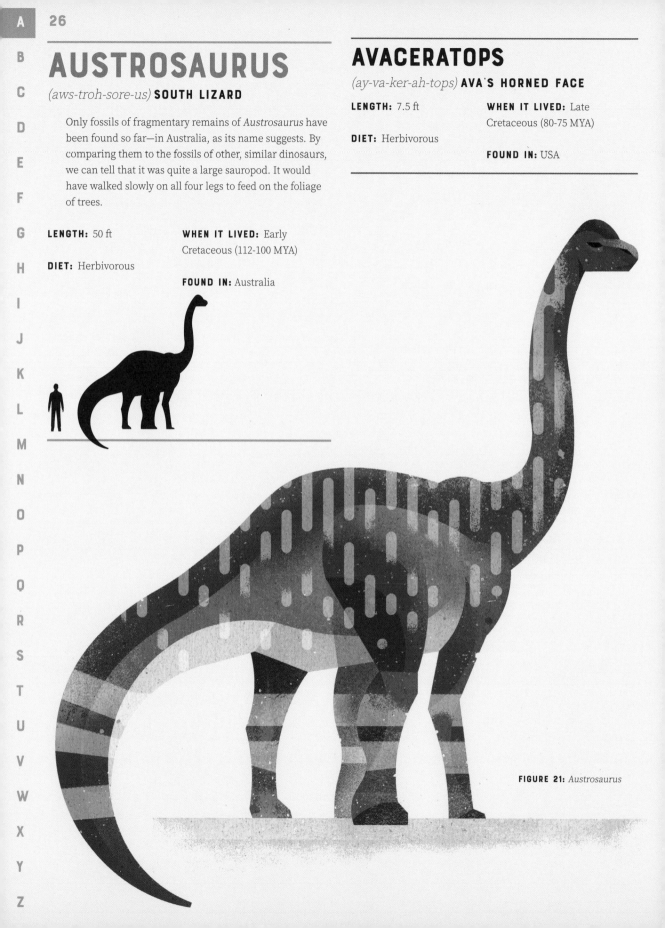

FIGURE 21: *Austrosaurus*

B C D E F G H I J K L M N O P Q R S T U V W X Y Z

AVIMIMUS

(ah-vee-mime-us) **BIRD MIMIC**

Avimimus was a close relative of *Oviraptor* (page 119) and probably had a similar mixed diet of plants, roots, seeds, and scavenged meat. Its name means "bird mimic" because it had many features that closely resemble modern birds: it had a very short tail compared with other bipedal dinosaurs, and had feathers on the lower part of its arms.

LENGTH: 5 ft

DIET: Omnivorous

WHEN IT LIVED: Late Cretaceous (80-75 MYA)

FOUND IN: People's Republic of China and Mongolia

AZENDOHSAURUS

(ah-zen-doh-sore-us) **AZENDOH LIZARD**

LENGTH: About 6 ft

DIET: Omnivorous

WHEN IT LIVED: Late Triassic (227-221 MYA)

FOUND IN: Morocco

FIGURE 22: *Avimimus*

B

BACTROSAURUS

(bak-troh-sore-us) **CLUB [SPINED] LIZARD**

Bactrosaurus was a medium-sized herbivore that lived in herds. Along with other members of its family, it would have performed a similar role to modern-day cows— moving across the land and eating low-lying plants. It had a line of club-shaped spines along its back and tail, which gave it its name.

LENGTH: 20 ft

DIET: Herbivorous

WHEN IT LIVED: Late Cretaceous (84-71 MYA)

FOUND IN: People's Republic of China

FIGURE 23: *Bactrosaurus*

BAGACERATOPS

(bag-a-ser-a-tops) **SMALL-HORNED FACE**

Bagaceratops was a very small dinosaur that spent most of its time chewing on low-lying vegetation. It belonged to the same family as *Triceratops* (page 165) but did not have the same elaborate head frill and horns, and did not grow to be as big.

LENGTH: 3 ft

DIET: Herbivorous

WHEN IT LIVED: Late Cretaceous (85-80 MYA)

FOUND IN: Mongolia

FIGURE 24: *Bagaceratops*

BAMBIRAPTOR

(bam-bee-rap-tor) **BAMBI PLUNDERER**

LENGTH: 3 ft

DIET: Carnivorous

WHEN IT LIVED: Late Cretaceous (84-71 MYA)

FOUND IN: USA

BARAPASAURUS

(bar-rap-oh-SORE-us) **BIG LEG LIZARD**

Barapasaurus was a very large, early sauropod. It lived at a time when long-necked sauropods were only just starting to grow from the size of the smaller two-legged dinosaurs like *Plateosaurus* (page 127) to be more like the later four-legged giant *Diplodocus* (page 55). *Barapasaurus* was somewhere in the middle of these two in size and weight, so knowing about this dinosaur helps scientists understand how the whole group would have changed over time.

LENGTH: 45 ft

DIET: Herbivorous

WHEN IT LIVED: Early Jurassic (185–170 MYA)

FOUND IN: India

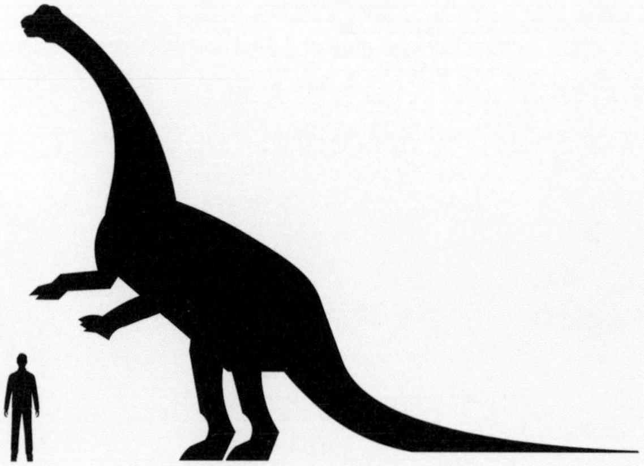

BARILIUM

(bar-ill-ee-um) **HEAVY ILLIUM**

LENGTH: 26-32 ft

DIET: Herbivorous

WHEN IT LIVED: Early Cretaceous (141-137 MYA)

FOUND IN: England

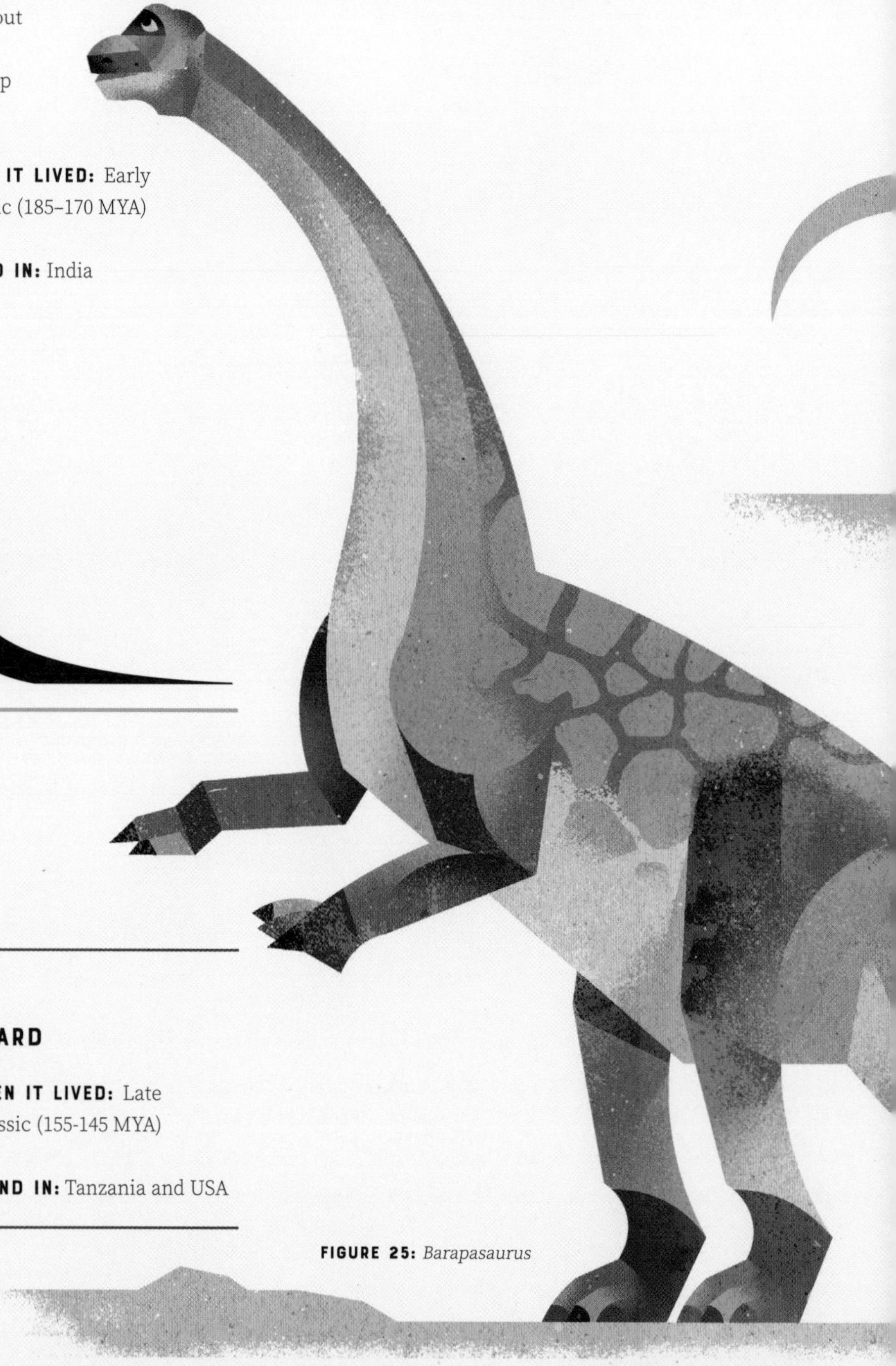

BAROSAURUS

(BAR-oh-sore-us) **HEAVY LIZARD**

LENGTH: 78 ft

DIET: Herbivorous

WHEN IT LIVED: Late Jurassic (155-145 MYA)

FOUND IN: Tanzania and USA

FIGURE 25: *Barapasaurus*

FIGURE 26: *Baryonyx*

BARYONYX

(bah-ree-ON-icks) **HEAVY CLAW**

This dinosaur's mouth shape was very similar to a crocodile's. It had a large claw—about 12 inches long—probably on its thumb. It may have crouched on riverbanks or waded through shallow water to hook fish with these claws, but it was also a scavenger, feasting on dead carcasses.

LENGTH: 32 ft

DIET: Carnivorous

WHEN IT LIVED: Early Cretaceous (125 MYA)

FOUND IN: England and Spain

BECKLESPINAX

(beck-el-spien-aks) **BECKLES' SPINAX**

LENGTH: About 16 ft

DIET: Carnivorous

WHEN IT LIVED: Early Cretaceous (142-132 MYA)

FOUND IN: England

BEIPIAOSAURUS

(bay-pyow-sore-us) **BEIPIAO LIZARD**

LENGTH: 6.5 ft

DIET: Omnivorous

WHEN IT LIVED: Early Cretaceous (127-121 MYA)

FOUND IN: People's Republic of China

BELLUSAURUS

(bel-uh-sore-us) **FINE LIZARD**

Discovered in 1990, this large plant-eater roamed the Jurassic plains of what is now China, clearing tree branches of leaves with its many flat teeth. It was by no means as large as some of the later sauropods, like *Diplodocus* (page 55), but it was still a heavy and slow-moving dinosaur.

LENGTH: 16 ft

DIET: Herbivorous

WHEN IT LIVED: Mid Jurassic (180-159 MYA)

FOUND IN: People's Republic of China

BOROGOVIA

(bor-o-goh-vee-a) **BOROGOVE**

Only the hindlimbs of this dinosaur have been found, so it is difficult to know what it really looked like. It was named after the borogroves in Lewis Carroll's 1871 "Jabberwocky" poem, which were fictional, shabby-looking birds.

LENGTH: 5 ft

DIET: Carnivorous

WHEN IT LIVED: Late Cretaceous (84-65 MYA)

FOUND IN: Mongolia

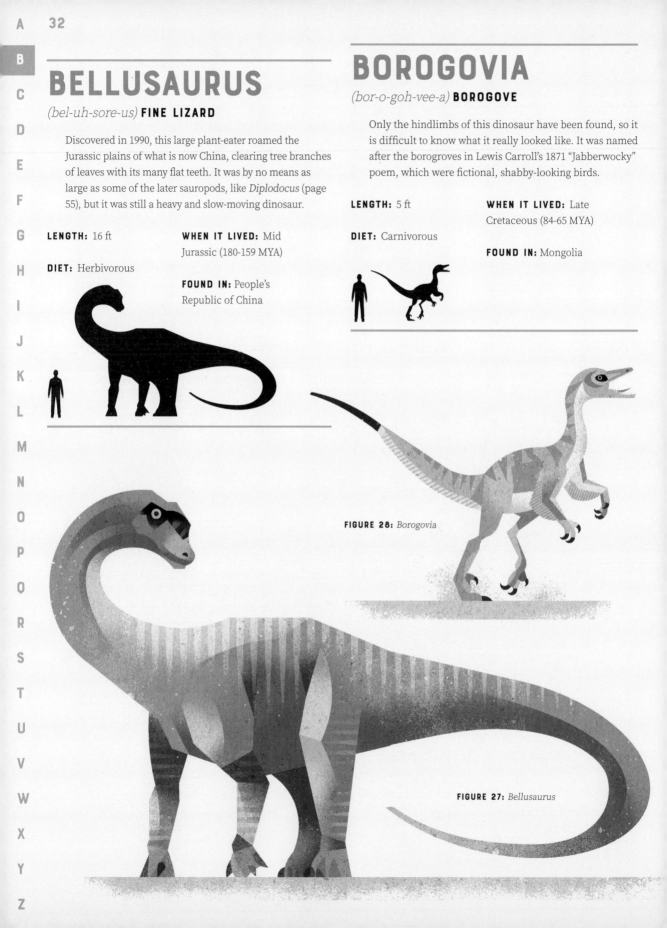

FIGURE 28: *Borogovia*

FIGURE 27: *Bellusaurus*

BRACHIOSAURUS

(BRAK-ee-oh-sore-us) **ARM LIZARD**

This long-necked dinosaur would have been the most spectacular sight on the plains of Late-Jurassic North America. As its legs were shorter than its arms, its body would have sloped upward toward the front, giving it a higher-reaching neck than other sauropods of the time. This meant *Brachiosaurus* could eat the highest leaves on trees, while the other sauropods like *Diplodocus* (page 55) ate the lower ones. This allowed them to live side by side without having to compete for food—something scientists call "niche partitioning."

LENGTH: 100 ft

DIET: Herbivorous

WHEN IT LIVED: Late Jurassic (155-140 MYA)

FOUND IN: Tanzania, USA, Portugal, and Algeria

FIGURE 29: *Brachiosaurus*

BRACHYCERATOPS

(brak-ee-ser-ah-tops) **SHORT-HORNED FACE**

Like *Bagaceratops* (page 29), this dinosaur was a smaller relative of the much bigger *Triceratops* (page 165). It had a frill on its head and a big nose horn, just like *Triceratops*, but it did not have the large horns above its eyes. Some scientists think the fossils of *Brachyceratops* are only from a juvenile, or it may just be the young of other species.

LENGTH: 6.5 ft

DIET: Herbivorous

WHEN IT LIVED: Late Cretaceous (81-74 MYA)

FOUND IN: USA

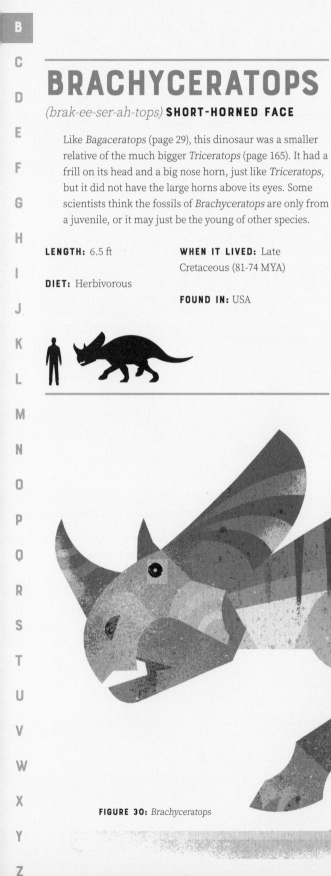

BRACHYLOPHOSAURUS

(brak-i-lof-oh-sore-us) **SHORT-CRESTED LIZARD**

LENGTH: 23 ft

DIET: Herbivorous

WHEN IT LIVED: Late Cretaceous (89-88 MYA)

FOUND IN: Canada and USA

FIGURE 30: *Brachyceratops*

FIGURE 31: *Brachytrachelopan*

BRACHYTRACHELOPAN

(brak-i-trak-eh-loh-pan)

SHORT-NECKED PAN [A SHEPHERD GOD]

Of all the sauropods, *Brachytrachelopan* had the shortest neck for a dinosaur of its size. It may have evolved to be that way so that it could feed on low- to medium-height plants that longer-necked dinosaurs may have overlooked.

LENGTH: 32 ft

DIET: Herbivorous

WHEN IT LIVED: Mid Jurassic (150 MYA)

FOUND IN: Argentina

A B C D E F G H I J K L M N O P Q R S T U V W X Y Z

BRONTOMERUS

(bron-toe-meh-rus) **THUNDER THIGH**

LENGTH: 50 ft

WHEN IT LIVED: Early Cretaceous (100-110 MYA)

DIET: Herbivorous

FOUND IN: USA

BUGENASAURA

(boo-jen-ah-sore-ah) **LARGE CHEEK LIZARD**

Bugenasaura was a plant-eating ornithopod (a dinosaur with hip bones shaped like a bird's) that looked very similar to *Thescelosaurus* (page 164). In fact, as these dinosaurs were so similar and came from the same place, some scientists think they are actually the same thing. If this turns out to be true, the name *Thescelosaurus* would be used instead of *Bugenasaura*.

LENGTH: 13 ft

WHEN IT LIVED: Late Cretaceous (65 MYA)

DIET: Herbivorous

FOUND IN: USA

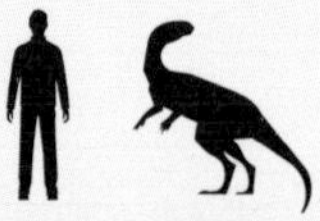

BUITRERAPTOR

(bwee-tree-rap-tor) **BUITRERA ("VULTURE ROOST") PLUNDERER**

LENGTH: 4 ft

WHEN IT LIVED: Late Cretaceous (99-90 MYA)

DIET: Carnivorous

FOUND IN: Argentina

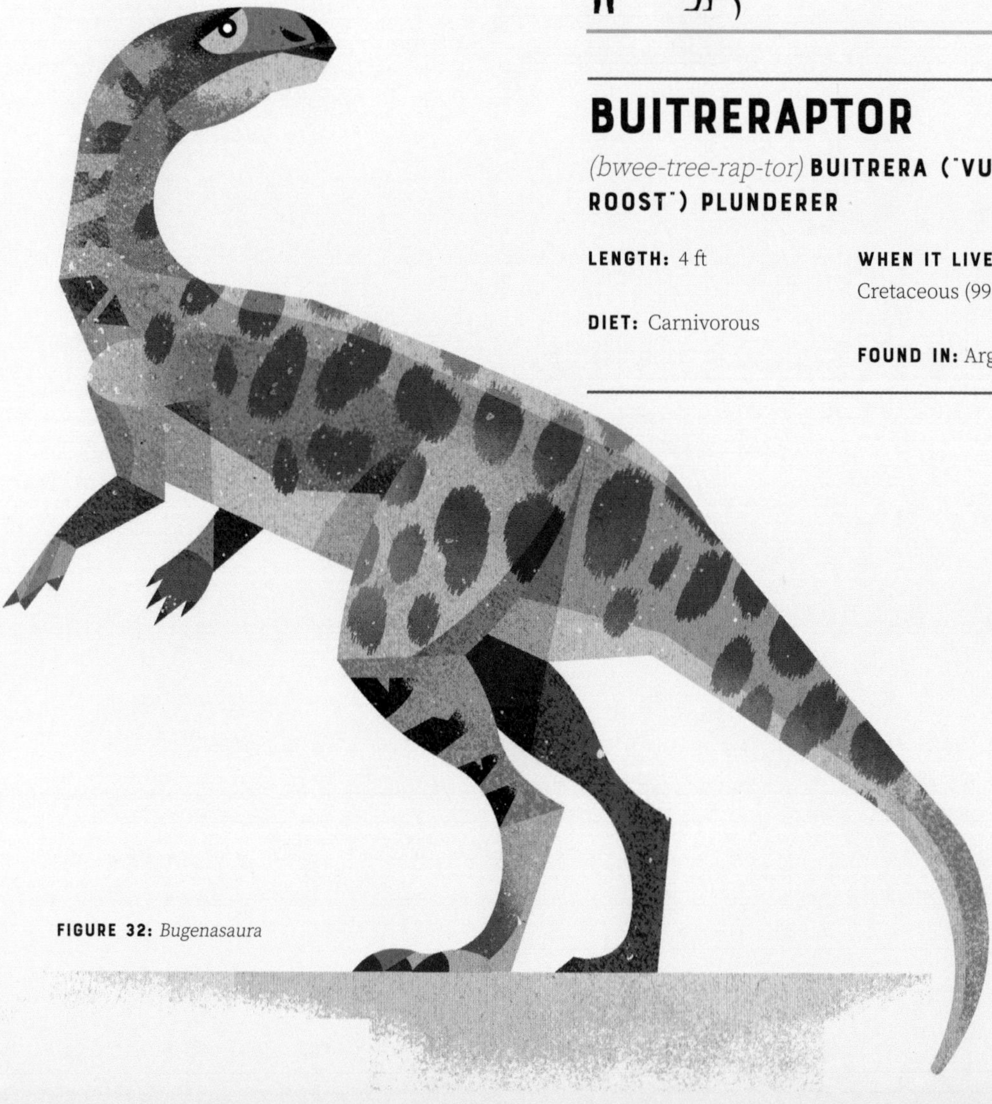

FIGURE 32: *Bugenasaura*

C - F

CAMARASAURUS

(KAM-ar-a-sore-us) **CHAMBERED LIZARD**

Camarasaurus was a large plant-eater with huge nostrils on each side of its head. It had hollow spaces inside the bones of its spine, which may have helped reduce its weight to make it easier for it to walk. It used its rows of close-set teeth to strip leaves from trees and shrubs, and swallowed "gizzard" stones to grind the leaves up in its stomach.

LENGTH: 75 ft

DIET: Herbivorous

WHEN IT LIVED: Late Jurassic (150-140 MYA)

FOUND IN: USA

CAMELOTIA

(cam-e-lo-te-a) **FROM CAMELOT**

LENGTH: 32 ft

DIET: Herbivorous

WHEN IT LIVED: Late Triassic and Early Jurassic (210-200 MYA)

FOUND IN: England

CAMPTOSAURUS

(KAMP-toe-sore-us) **BENT LIZARD**

LENGTH: 16 ft

DIET: Herbivorous

WHEN IT LIVED: Late Jurassic (155-145 MYA)

FOUND IN: England and USA

FIGURE 33: *Camarasaurus*

FIGURE 34: *Carnotaurus*

CARNOTAURUS

(Kar-noh-TORE-us) **CARNIVOROUS BULL**

Carnotaurus was a fearsome meat-eating dinosaur. It had big horns above its eyes—like a bull—which is where it gets its name: *taurus* means "bull." The horns were probably for display, either to attract a mate or to scare away rivals.

LENGTH: 25 ft

DIET: Carnivorous

WHEN IT LIVED: Late Cretaceous (70 MYA)

FOUND IN: Argentina

CARCHARODONTOSAURUS

(Kar-KAR-o-don-toe-sore-us) **CARCHARODON LIZARD**

LENGTH: About 50 ft

DIET: Carnivorous

WHEN IT LIVED: Late Cretaceous (98-94 MYA)

FOUND IN: North Africa

CEDARPELTA

(see-dar-pel-tuh)
CEDAR [A MOUNTAIN FORMATION] SHIELD

LENGTH: 32 ft

DIET: Herbivorous

WHEN IT LIVED: Early Cretaceous (142-127 MYA)

FOUND IN: USA

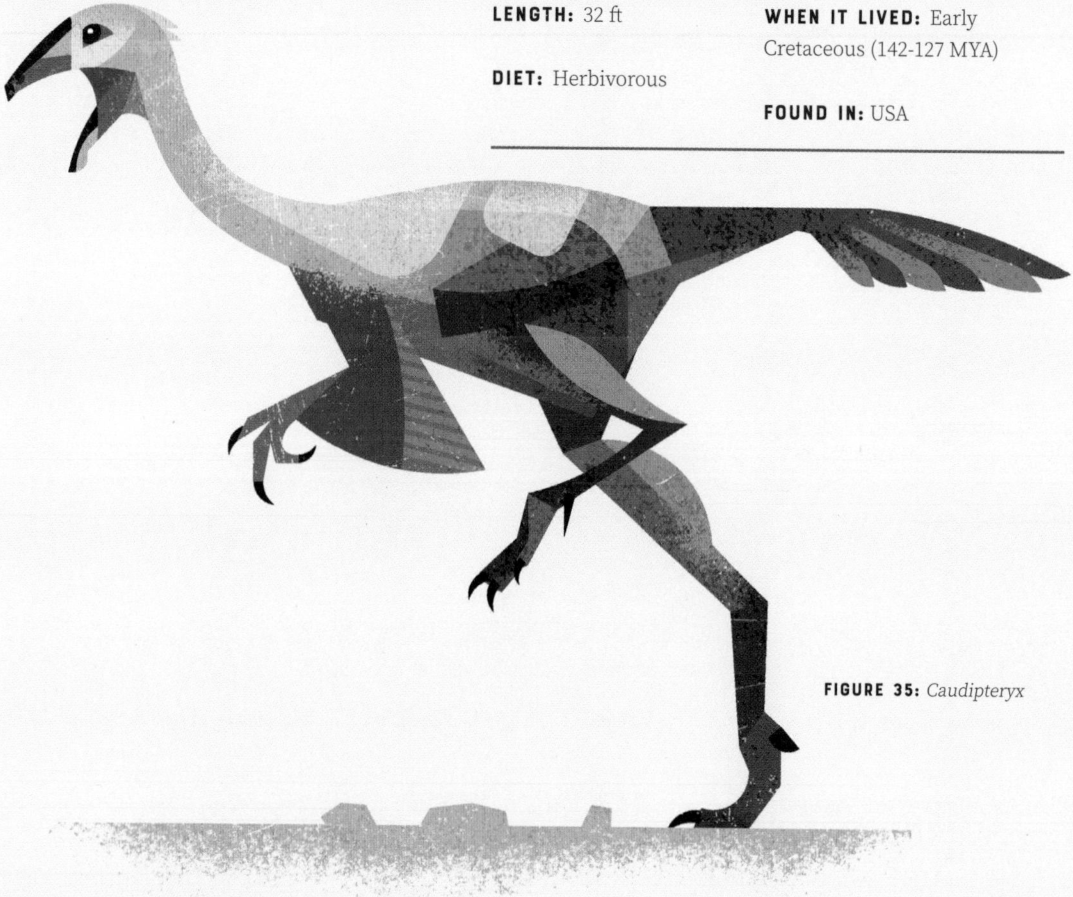

FIGURE 35: *Caudipteryx*

CAUDIPTERYX

(caw-dip-ter-iks) **TAIL FEATHER**

As a birdlike dinosaur, *Caudipteryx* had a fan of feathers at the end of its tail. Fossils of this dinosaur have been found with "gizzard" stones in its stomach, which it may have swallowed to help it digest food. It had small, weak teeth and probably ate both insects and plants.

LENGTH: 3 ft

DIET: Omnivorous

WHEN IT LIVED: Early Cretaceous (125-122 MYA)

FOUND IN: People's Republic of China

CENTROSAURUS

(cen-TROH-sore-us) **SHARP-POINTED LIZARD**

LENGTH: 20 ft

DIET: Herbivorous

WHEN IT LIVED: Late Cretaceous (76-74 MYA)

FOUND IN: Canada

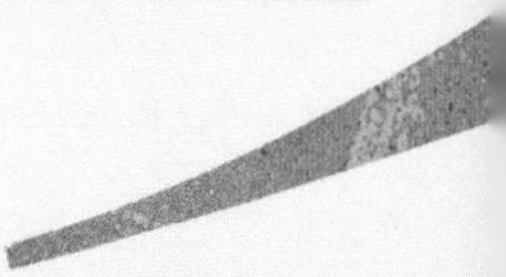

CERATOSAURUS

(Keh-RAT-oh-sore-us) **HORNED LIZARD**

Ceratosaurus was one of the biggest hunters in the Jurassic Period. Its name means "horned lizard" because it had a row of sharp horns on its head and also a row of small, bony pieces of armor running along its back. It is not known what this body armor was for, but it could have been for protection from attack by other *Ceratosaurus*.

LENGTH: 20 ft

DIET: Carnivorous

WHEN IT LIVED: Late Jurassic (150-144 MYA)

FOUND IN: USA

FIGURE 36: *Ceratosaurus*

A
B
C
D
E
F
G
H
I
J
K
L
M
N
O
P
Q
R
S
T
U
V
W
X
Y
Z

CHAOYANGSAURUS

(chow-yahng-sore-us) **CHAOYANG LIZARD**

Chaoyangsaurus is the earliest known dinosaur from the same group as *Triceratops* (page 165)—the ceratopsians (meaning "shield" dinosaur). A very small dinosaur, it probably walked on two legs and lacked the large horns and neck frills of later ceratopsians.

LENGTH: 3.5 ft

DIET: Herbivorous

WHEN IT LIVED: Late Jurassic (150-148 MYA)

FOUND IN: People's Republic of China

CETIOSAURISCUS

(see-tee-oh-SORE-is-kuss) **LIKE WHALE LIZARD**

LENGTH: 50 ft

DIET: Herbivorous

WHEN IT LIVED: Mid Jurassic (175-160 MYA)

FOUND IN: England

FIGURE 37: *Chaoyangsaurus*

FIGURE 38: *Chasmosaurus*

CHASMOSAURUS

(KAZ-mo-sore-us) **CHASM LIZARD**

Chasmosaurus would have shared similarities with today's rhinoceros. It had a small nose horn, blunt brow horns, and a long neck frill with holes. This dinosaur may have been quite social—traveling in large herds and caring for its young. It probably protected itself by charging at a threat at full speed—much like a rhinoceros does.

LENGTH: 16 ft

DIET: Herbivorous

WHEN IT LIVED: Late Cretaceous (76-74 MYA)

FOUND IN: Canada

CHIALINGOSAURUS

(jyah-ling-oh-sore-us) **JIALING [RIVER] LIZARD**

LENGTH: 13 ft

DIET: Herbivorous

WHEN IT LIVED: Late Jurassic (159-142 MYA)

FOUND IN: People's Republic of China

CHINDESAURUS

(chin-dee-sore-us) **CHINDE LIZARD**

Chindesaurus had a long, whiplike tail and tall legs. It is a very mysterious early hunter, as not much fossil material has been found. Some scientists think it is closely related to *Herrerasaurus* (page 78) from Argentina, while others think it is more closely related to *Coelophysis* (page 46) from America. Either way, we can be certain that it was a fast-running, two-legged meat-eater.

LENGTH: 13 ft

DIET: Carnivorous

WHEN IT LIVED: Late Triassic (227-210 MYA)

FOUND IN: USA

FIGURE 39: *Chindesaurus*

CHINSHAKIANGOSAURUS

(jing-sha-kiang-oh-sore-us) **CHINSHAKIANG LIZARD**

Not much is known about *Chinshakiangosaurus*, as so little fossil material exists. Based on the structure of its mouth, this small sauropod was likely very selective about the foliage it ate, whereas later, larger sauropods were less selective and probably grabbed big mouthfuls of food.

LENGTH: 36-43 ft

DIET: Herbivorous

WHEN IT LIVED: Late Jurassic (159-142 MYA)

FOUND IN: People's Republic of China

FIGURE 40: *Chinshakiangosaurus*

CHIROSTENOTES

(kie-ro-sten-oh-teez) **NARROW HANDED**

LENGTH: 5.5-6.5 ft

DIET: Omnivorous

WHEN IT LIVED: Late Cretaceous (79-67 MYA)

FOUND IN: Canada

CHUBUTISAURUS

(choo-boot-i-sore-us) **CHUBUT [PROVINCE] LIZARD**

LENGTH: 75 ft

DIET: Herbivorous

WHEN IT LIVED: Early Cretaceous (112-100 MYA)

FOUND IN: Argentina

FIGURE 41: *Chungkingosaurus*

CHUNGKINGOSAURUS

(chung-ching-oh-sore-us) **CHONGQING LIZARD**

Chungkingosaurus was a stegosaur (dinosaurs with rows of bony plates on their backs), like *Stegosaurus* (page 153). It almost certainly had spikes at the end of its tail, but these were shorter than on other stegosaurs, which suggests that they might not have been as useful to *Chungkingosaurus* for defending itself.

LENGTH: 13 ft

DIET: Herbivorous

WHEN IT LIVED: Late Jurassic (159-142 MYA)

FOUND IN: People's Republic of China

FIGURE 42: *Coelophysis*

COELOPHYSIS

(seel-OH-fie-sis) **HOLLOW FORM**

Coelophysis had hollow limb bones, which would have given it a light body—best-suited to a swift and agile hunter. Early meat-eating dinosaurs like this relied on their speed to catch animals such as insects and small reptiles, and its sharp teeth and grasping claws would have helped it hold and kill its food.

LENGTH: 10 ft

DIET: Carnivorous

WHEN IT LIVED: Late Triassic (225-220 MYA)

FOUND IN: USA

CITIPATI

(chit-i-puh-tih) **LORD OF THE FUNERAL PYRE**

LENGTH: 7 ft

DIET: Omnivorous

WHEN IT LIVED: Late Cretaceous (81-75 MYA)

FOUND IN: Mongolia

FIGURE 43: *Compsognathus*

COELURUS

(seel-YEW-rus) **HOLLOW TAIL**

LENGTH: 6 ft

DIET: Carnivorous

WHEN IT LIVED: Late Jurassic (155-145 MYA)

FOUND IN: USA

COLORADISAURUS

(ko-lo-rahd-i-sore-us) **[LOS] COLORADOS LIZARD**

LENGTH: About 13 ft

DIET: Omnivorous

WHEN IT LIVED: Late Triassic (221-210 MYA)

FOUND IN: Argentina

COMPSOGNATHUS

(komp-sog-NATH-us) **PRETTY JAW**

Compsognathus was a meat-eating dinosaur that was only about as tall as a chicken. Sometimes nicknamed "compys," these little animals would have relied on their speed and quick reflexes to hunt in the Late Jurassic. In fact, a little reptile called *Bavarisaurus* was once found inside the belly of a *Compsognathus*, giving scientists an important clue about what this dinosaur hunted.

LENGTH: 2 ft

DIET: Carnivorous

WHEN IT LIVED: Late Jurassic (150 MYA)

FOUND IN: Germany and France

FIGURE 44: *Conchoraptor*

CONCHORAPTOR

(kon-koh-rap-tor) **CONCH THIEF**

Conchoraptor is named the "mussel thief" because some scientists believe that it may have eaten mussels and other shelled mollusks, using its beak to crack them open. Remains of *Conchoraptor* have been found with its feathers preserved, showing that females and males might've had different plumage.

LENGTH: 5 ft

DIET: Carnivorous

WHEN IT LIVED: Late Cretaceous (81-76 MYA)

FOUND IN: Mongolia

CONFUCIUSORNIS

(kon-few-shus-or-niss) **CONFUCIUS BIRD**

LENGTH: 10 in

DIET: Carnivorous

WHEN IT LIVED: Early Cretaceous (127-121 MYA)

FOUND IN: People's Republic of China

FIGURE 45: *Corythosaurus*

CORYTHOSAURUS

(koh-rith-OH-sore-us)

CORINTHIAN HELMET LIZARD

Corythosaurus had a big duck-bill on the end of its skull, and a large crest on top. The crest was probably for display and signaling to other members of its species. Like other hadrosaurs, *Corythosaurus* ate only plants. It was probably hunted by the big predators of its time—like *Daspletosaurus* (page 51).

LENGTH: 32 ft

WHEN IT LIVED: Late Cretaceous (76-74 MYA)

DIET: Herbivorous

FOUND IN: Canada and USA

CRYOLOPHOSAURUS

(cry-o-loaf-oh-sore-us) **FROZEN-CRESTED LIZARD**

LENGTH: 26 ft

DIET: Carnivorous

WHEN IT LIVED: Early Jurassic (170 MYA)

FOUND IN: Antarctica

FIGURE 46: *Dacentrurus*

D

DACENTRURUS

(dah-sen-troo-russ) **POINTED TAIL**

Dacentrurus was the first stegosaur ever discovered. It was originally called *Omosaurus,* but that turned out to be a mistake—as a crocodile species had already been given that name before. Like other stegosaurs, it probably had large spines or plates running along its back and a set of spikes on its tail called a "thagomizer."

LENGTH: 20 ft

DIET: Herbivorous

WHEN IT LIVED: Late Jurassic (154-150 MYA)

FOUND IN: England, Portugal, and France

DASPLETOSAURUS

(da-PLEE-toe-SORE-us) **FRIGHTFUL LIZARD**

Daspletosaurus was a very large predator and a close relative of *Tyrannosaurus* (page 169)—so close that, for a long time, scientists thought the two were the same thing. Now we know that *Daspletosaurus* and *Tyrannosaurus* are different species, and that *Daspletosaurus* evolved 10 million years before its cousin. They would have fought each other for food, territory, and dominance, until *Tyrannosaurus* replaced *Daspletosaurus*.

LENGTH: 30 ft

WHEN IT LIVED: Late Cretaceous (76-74 MYA)

DIET: Carnivorous

FOUND IN: Canada

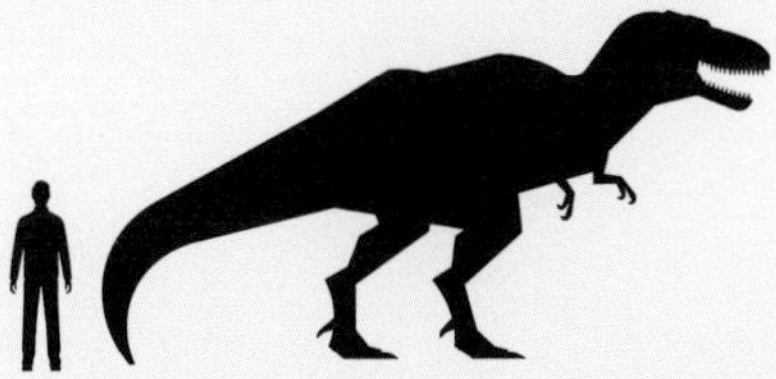

DATOUSAURUS

(dah-too-sore-us) **DATOU LIZARD**

LENGTH: 50-65 ft

DIET: Herbivorous

WHEN IT LIVED: Middle Jurassic (160 MYA)

FOUND IN: People's Republic of China

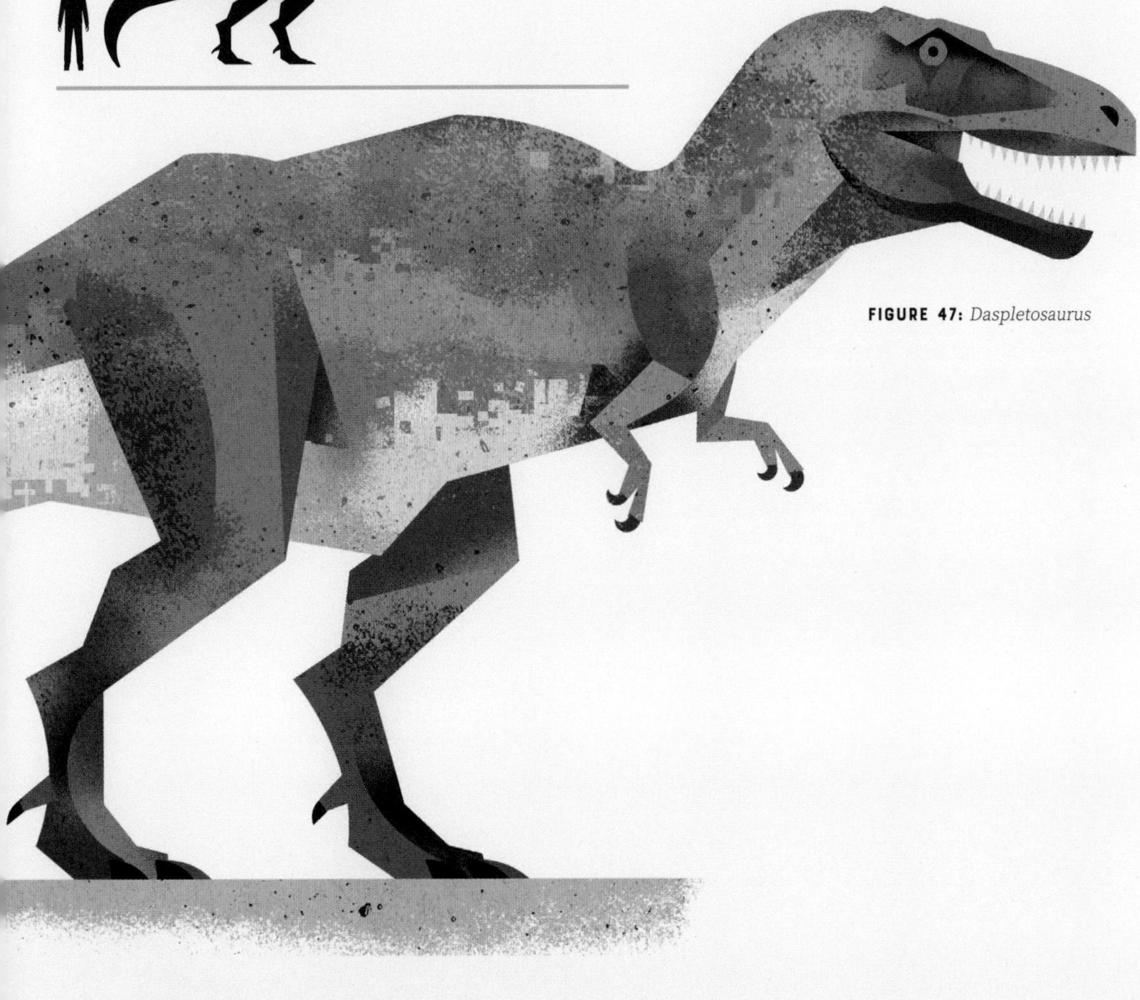

FIGURE 47: *Daspletosaurus*

A B C D E F G H I J K L M N O P Q R S T U V W X Y Z

FIGURE 48: *Deinocheirus*

DEINOCHEIRUS

(DINE-oh-KIRE-us) **TERRIBLE HAND**

Originally, scientists only had a pair of arm bones with big, long claws to learn about *Deinocheirus*. But in 2014, new material revealed that it had a unique, large hump on its back, supported by its back bones. Now we know that it was a truly bizarre-looking creature, with huge, clawed hands, a beaked head like a duck, and a hump like a camel.

LENGTH: 32 ft

DIET: Omivorous

WHEN IT LIVED: Late Cretaceous (70-65 MYA)

FOUND IN: Mongolia

DEINONYCHUS

(die-non-ick-us) **TERRIBLE CLAW**

LENGTH: About 10 ft

DIET: Carnivorous

WHEN IT LIVED: Cretaceous (125-100 MYA)

FOUND IN: USA

DELTADROMEUS

(del-tah-dor-me-us) **DELTA RUNNER**

LENGTH: 32 ft

DIET: Carnivorous

WHEN IT LIVED: Cretaceous (95 MYA)

FOUND IN: Northern Africa

DIAMANTINASAURUS

(die-a-man-TEEN-a-SORE-us)

DIAMANTINA RIVER LIZARD

So far, the few fossils that have been found of *Diamantinasaurus* show that it was a titanosaur—which was an enormous sauropod. However, *Diamantinasaurus* would have been rather small compared to other titanosaurs, which could grow to be a whole 65 feet longer. The fossils of *Diamantinasaurus* also show it had a thumb claw, which is unusual for a titanosaur. Although it has been described by some as being stocky and resembling a giant hippo, *Diamantinasaurus* would have lived on land—not in water.

LENGTH: 50-53 ft

DIET: Herbivore

WHEN IT LIVED: Late Cretaceous (94-90 MYA)

FOUND IN: Australia

FIGURE 49: *Diamantinasaurus*

DICRAEOSAURUS

(die-KRAY-oh-SORE-us) **FORKED LIZARD**

LENGTH: 65 ft

DIET: Herbivorous

WHEN IT LIVED: Late Jurassic (150-135 MYA)

FOUND IN: Tanzania

DILONG

(dee-long) **EMPEROR DRAGON**

LENGTH: Over 6.5 ft

DIET: Carnivorous

WHEN IT LIVED: Early Cretaceous (125 MYA)

FOUND IN: People's Republic of China

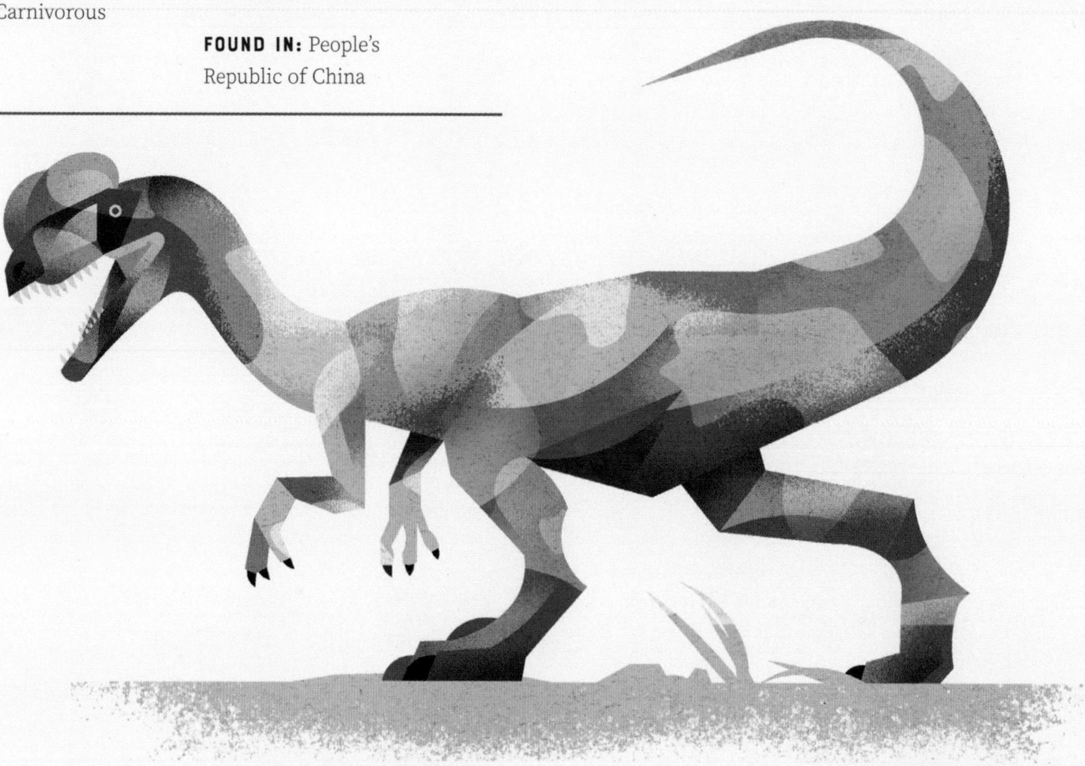

FIGURE 50: *Dilophosaurus*

DILOPHOSAURUS

(die-LOAF-oh-sore-us) **TWO-RIDGED LIZARD**

Dilophosaurus was a fast-moving meat-eater. A pair of thin, bony crests on its head may have been for display, while a kink in its upper jaw could either mean that it ate a certain kind of food, or that it attacked its prey by gripping and holding on to it—much like crocodiles do.

LENGTH: 20 ft

DIET: Carnivorous

WHEN IT LIVED: Early Jurassic (190 MYA)

FOUND IN: USA

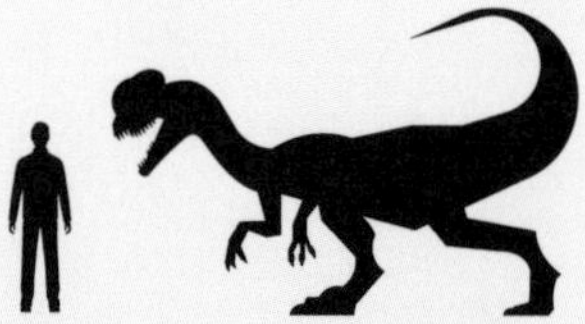

FIGURE 51: *Diplodocus*

DIPLODOCUS

(DIP-low DOCK-us) **DOUBLE BEAM**

Diplodocus had a long neck that it would have used to reach high and low vegetation, and to drink water. Its front limbs were shorter than its back legs, so it would have had a horizontal posture. It probably had narrow, pointed bony spines lining its back, and could have waved its tail around like a powerful whip. It is hard to imagine the enormous amount of vegetation a creature of this size would have eaten.

LENGTH: 85 ft

DIET: Herbivorous

WHEN IT LIVED: Late Jurassic (155-145 MYA)

FOUND IN: USA

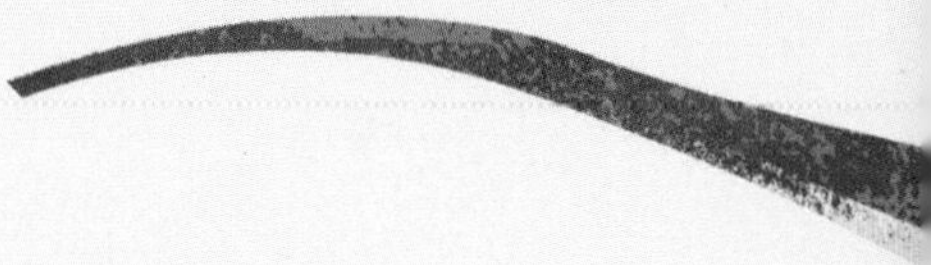

DRACOREX

(dray-ko-rex) **DRAGON KING**

LENGTH: 13 ft

WHEN IT LIVED: Late Cretaceous (66 MYA)

DIET: Herbivorous

FOUND IN: USA

DRAVIDOSAURUS

(dra-vid-oh-sore-us) **DRAVIDANADU LIZARD**

The original fossil that was used to identify this dinosaur was once thought to be from a marine reptile—known as a plesiosaur. But *Dravidosaurus* is now thought to be a stegosaur. However, scientists still disagree about this, so until more information comes to light, its place in the prehistoric family tree remains a mystery.

LENGTH: 10 ft

WHEN IT LIVED: Late Cretaceous (89-86 MYA)

DIET: Herbivorous

FOUND IN: India

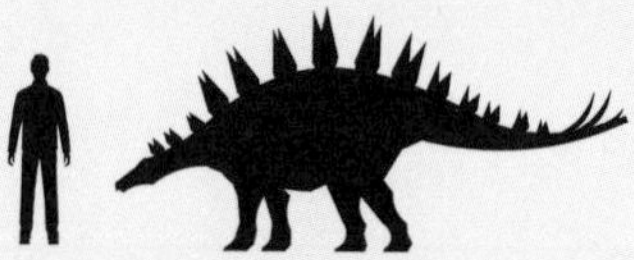

DROMAEOSAURUS

(DROM-ee-oh-saw-russ) **RUNNING LIZARD**

LENGTH: 6 ft

WHEN IT LIVED: Late Cretaceous (76-74 MYA)

DIET: Carnivorous

FOUND IN: Canada and USA

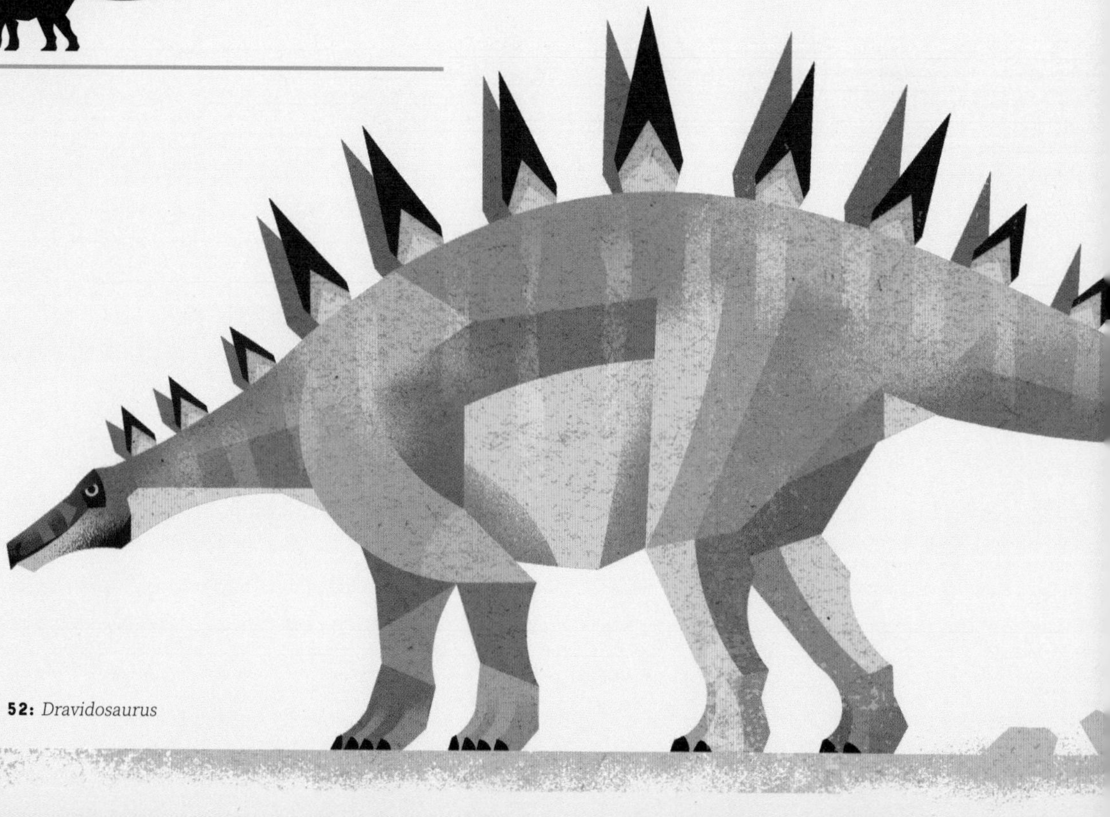

FIGURE 52: *Dravidosaurus*

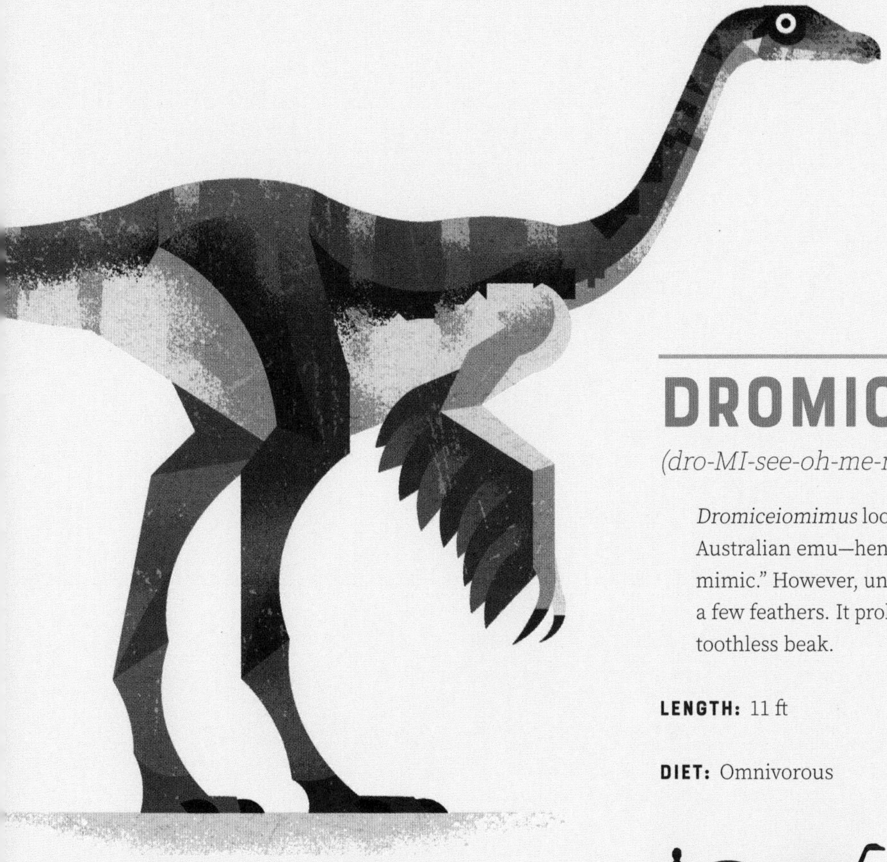

FIGURE 53: *Dromiceiomimus*

DROMICEIOMIMUS

(dro-MI-see-oh-me-muss) **EMU MIMIC**

Dromiceiomimus looked very much like a modern Australian emu—hence the name, which means "emu mimic." However, unlike the emu, it may have had only a few feathers. It probably walked on two legs and had a toothless beak.

LENGTH: 11 ft

DIET: Omnivorous

WHEN IT LIVED: Late Cretaceous (74-70 MYA)

FOUND IN: Canada

DRYOSAURUS

(dry-oh-SORE-us) **OAK LIZARD**

LENGTH: 13 ft

DIET: Herbivorous

WHEN IT LIVED: Late Jurassic (155-140 MYA)

FOUND IN: Tanzania and USA

DRYPTOSAURUS

(drip-toe-SORE-us) **TEARING LIZARD**

LENGTH: 13 ft

DIET: Carnivorous

WHEN IT LIVED: Late Cretaceous (84-65 MYA)

FOUND IN: USA

FIGURE 54: *Dubreuillosaurus*

DUBREUILLOSAURUS

(dub-rhe-oo-oh-sore-us) **DUBREUIL'S LIZARD**

Dubreuillosaurus was a carnivore, and probably very closely related to *Megalosaurus* (page 103). Only fragments of the skull and skeleton of *Dubreuillosaurus* have been found. Because this dinosaur was found in rocks along the coast, it is possible that it hunted fish like its cousin *Spinosaurus* (page 151).

LENGTH: 26 ft

DIET: Carnivorous

WHEN IT LIVED: Late Jurassic (169-164 MYA)

FOUND IN: France

DURIATITAN

(dure-E-a-tie-tan) **DORSET TITAN**

LENGTH: 60-82 ft

DIET: Herbivore

WHEN IT LIVED: Late Jurassic (155-150 MYA)

FOUND IN: England

A
B
C
D
E
F
G
H
I
J
K
L
M
N
O
P
Q
R
S
T
U
V
W
X
Y
Z

EDMONTOSAURUS

(ed-MON-toe-sore-us) **EDMONTON LIZARD**

This large animal is named after the Canadian state of Edmonton, where it was discovered. Hard conifer needles, twigs, and seeds have all been found in *Edmontosaurus's* stomach. It may have had an inflatable area around its nostrils which it could use to make sounds for communication. Incredibly, some fossils are so well preserved that they show the texture of *Edmontosaurus's* skin.

LENGTH: 43 ft

DIET: Herbivorous

WHEN IT LIVED: Late Cretaceous (76-65 MYA)

FOUND IN: Canada

DURIAVENATOR

(dure-ee-a-ven-a-tor) **DORSET HUNTER**

LENGTH: 20-23 ft

DIET: Carnivorous

WHEN IT LIVED: Middle Jurassic (170 MYA)

FOUND IN: England

FIGURE 55: *Edmontosaurus*

EDMONTONIA

(ed-mon-TONE-ee-ah) **OF EDMONTON**

LENGTH: 13 ft

DIET: Herbivorous

WHEN IT LIVED: Late Cretaceous (76-74 MYA)

FOUND IN: Canada

EINIOSAURUS

(ie-nee-oh-sore-us) **BISON LIZARD**

LENGTH: 20 ft

DIET: Herbivorous

WHEN IT LIVED: Late Cretaceous (74 MYA)

FOUND IN: USA

ELAPHROSAURUS

(el-a-fro-sore-us) **FLEET LIZARD**

LENGTH: 20 ft

DIET: Carnivorous

WHEN IT LIVED: Late Jurassic (154-151 MYA)

FOUND IN: Tanzania

EMAUSAURUS

(em-ow-sore-us)

ERNST-MORITZ-ARNDT-UNIVERSITÄT LIZARD

Emausaurus was a small herbivore that would have eaten plants close to the ground. It was covered in bony scutes (horned plates or scales) to prevent predators from biting into its skin.

LENGTH: 6.5 ft

DIET: Herbivorous

WHEN IT LIVED: Mid Jurassic (190-180 MYA)

FOUND IN: Germany

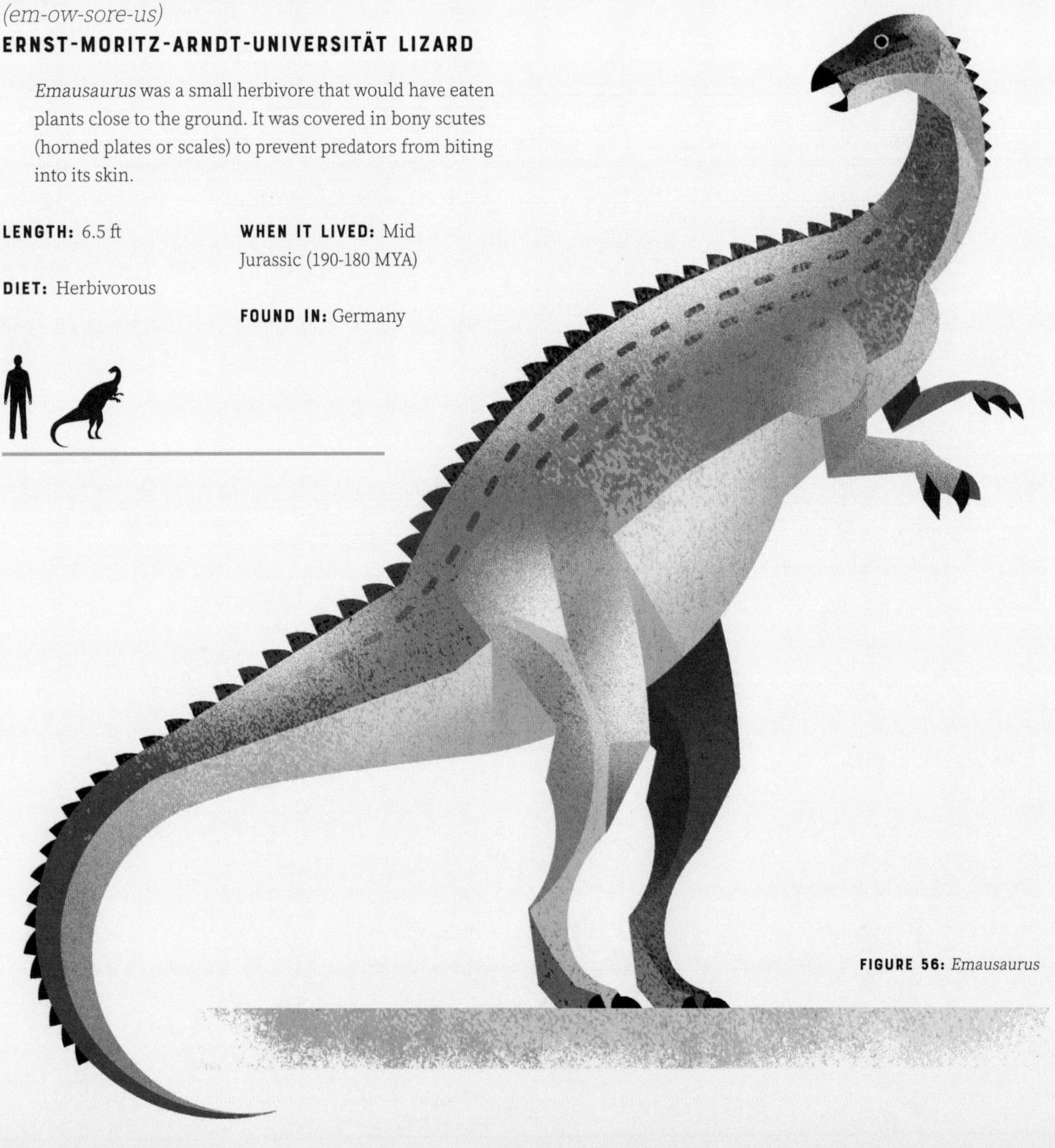

FIGURE 56: *Emausaurus*

EODROMAEUS

(EE-oh-DROHM-ee-us) **DAWN RUNNER**

LENGTH: 5 ft

DIET: Carnivorous

WHEN IT LIVED: Late Triassic (230 MYA)

FOUND IN: Argentina

FIGURE 57: *Eolambia*

EOLAMBIA

(ee-oh-lam-bee-ah) **DAWN LAMBEOSAURINE**

Eolambia was a medium-sized hadrosaur (a type of dinosaur with a flat, duck-billed snout), which ate plants using its beak. "Eo" means "dawn," so its name refers to the fact that it came before the lambeosaur dinosaurs—a group of hadrosaurs that had hollow crests on their heads.

LENGTH: 20 ft

DIET: Herbivorous

WHEN IT LIVED: Late Cretaceous (99-94 MYA)

FOUND IN: USA

EORAPTOR

(EE-oh-RAP-tor) **EARLY PLUNDERER**

LENGTH: 3 ft

DIET: Carnivorous

WHEN IT LIVED: Late Triassic (228 MYA)

FOUND IN: Argentina

EOTYRANNUS

(ee-oh-ti-ran-us) **DAWN TYRANT**

LENGTH: 16 ft

DIET: Carnivorous

WHEN IT LIVED: Early Cretaceous (127-121 MYA)

FOUND IN: England

A
B
C
D
E
F
G
H
I
J
K
L
M
N
O
P
Q
R
S
T
U
V
W
X
Y
Z

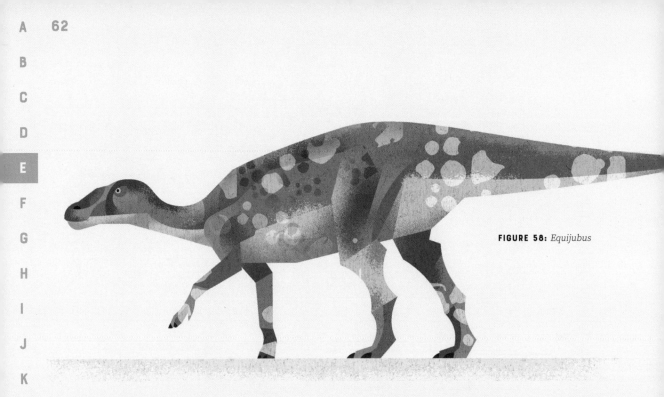

FIGURE 58: *Equijubus*

EQUIJUBUS

(ee-kwee-joo-bus) **HORSE MANE**

Fossils of *Equijubus* have been found in Asia, and it is thought to have been the earliest of the hadrosaurs to walk the Earth. This means hadrosaurs probably evolved in Asia before later migrating out to North America. *Equijubus* lived on a diet of plants and used its big beak to crop vegetation.

LENGTH: 23-26 ft

DIET: Herbivorous

WHEN IT LIVED: Early Cretaceous (127-99 MYA)

FOUND IN: People's Republic of China

ERKETU

(er-kee-tu) **TENGRI (A MONGOLIAN CREATOR-GOD)**

LENGTH: 50 ft

DIET: Herbivorous

WHEN IT LIVED: Early Cretaceous (100-83 MYA)

FOUND IN: Mongolia

ERLIKOSAURUS

(er-lik-oh-sore-us) **ERLIK'S LIZARD**

Erlikosaurus was a bizarre-looking dinosaur. Although it belongs to a group of dinosaurs known as theropods (dinosaurs with short arms that walked on two legs)—which normally only ate meat—it had a big, round potbelly for digesting plants instead. It probably looked a bit like *Deinonychus* (page 52), but with big claws and smaller teeth.

LENGTH: 11 ft

DIET: Omnivorous

WHEN IT LIVED: Late Cretaceous (99-89 MYA)

FOUND IN: Mongolia

EUHELOPUS

(yoo-hel-oh-pus) **TRUE MARSH FOOT**

LENGTH: 32-50 ft

DIET: Herbivorous

WHEN IT LIVED: Late Jurassic (154-142 MYA)

FOUND IN: People's Republic of China

FIGURE 59: *Erlikosaurus*

EUOPLOCEPHALUS

(you-OH-plo-kef-ah-luss) **WELL-ARMORED HEAD**

Euoplocephalus had bony spikes and armor plating on its back, and a bony tail club. It was an ankylosaur, so it had a short, fat head covered in armor to protect it from attack. Despite being big, this dinosaur only had a very small brain, and would not have done much in life beyond grazing vegetation with other members of its species.

LENGTH: 23 ft

DIET: Herbivorous

WHEN IT LIVED: Late Cretaceous (76-70 MYA)

FOUND IN: Canada and USA

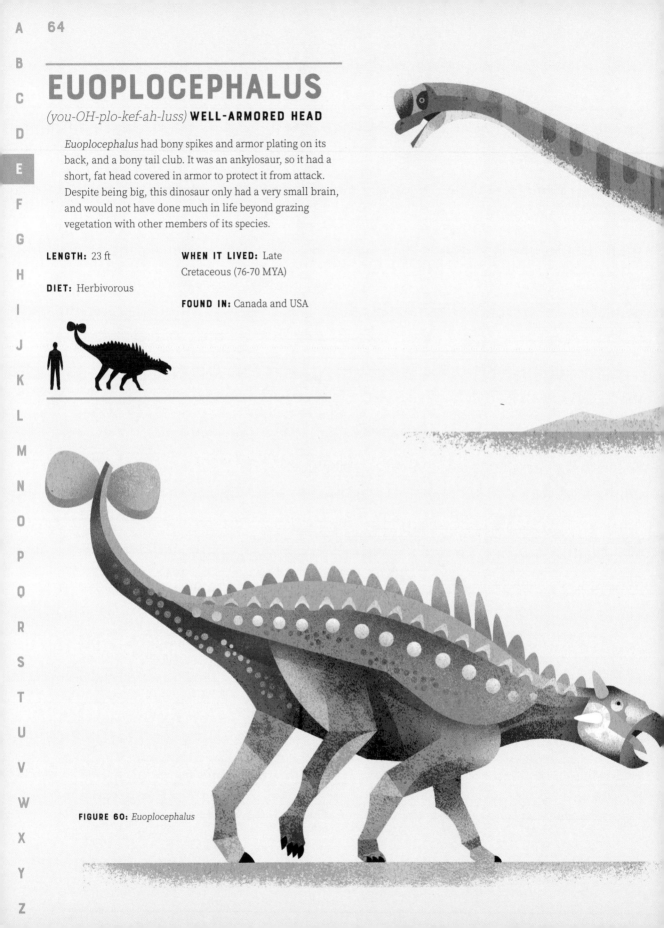

FIGURE 60: *Euoplocephalus*

FIGURE 61: *Europasaurus*

EUROPASAURUS

(yoo-roh-pah-sore-us) **EUROPE LIZARD**

Although *Europasaurus* was a dwarf sauropod, it still grew to about 20 feet long. It was one of the "big-nosed" sauropod dinosaurs that scientists call macronarians. This is because the openings of their noses were huge and high up on their heads. Like all other sauropods, *Europasaurus* only ate plants.

LENGTH: 20 ft

DIET: Herbivorous

WHEN IT LIVED: Late Jurassic (154-151 MYA)

FOUND IN: Germany

EUSKELOSAURUS

(yoo-skeel-oh-sore-us) **TRUE-LIMBED LIZARD**

LENGTH: 32 ft

DIET: Omnivorous

WHEN IT LIVED: Late Triassic (227-210 MYA)

FOUND IN: Lesotho, South Africa and Zimbabwe

EUSTREPTOSPONDYLUS

(ewe-strep-toe-SPON-die-luss)
WELL-CURVED VERTEBRA

LENGTH: 23 ft

DIET: Carnivorous

WHEN IT LIVED: Mid Jurassic (165 MYA)

FOUND IN: England

F

FUKUIRAPTOR

(foo-koo-ee-rap-tor) **FUKUI PLUNDERER**

Fukuiraptor was a medium- to large-sized meat-eater from Japan. Many fossils have been found since its original discovery, but some of them are much smaller than the first one, suggesting that they are juveniles. *Fukuiraptor* was a hunter, with three claws on its hands and sharp teeth for tearing meat. It probably hunted *Fukuisaurus* (page 66).

LENGTH: 14 ft

DIET: Carnivorous

WHEN IT LIVED: Early Cretaceous (121-99 MYA)

FOUND IN: Japan

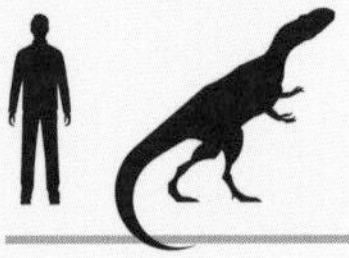

FUKUISAURUS

(foo-koo-I-sore-us) **FUKUI LIZARD**

LENGTH: 15 ft

DIET: Herbivorous

WHEN IT LIVED: Early Cretaceous (121-99 MYA)

FOUND IN: Japan

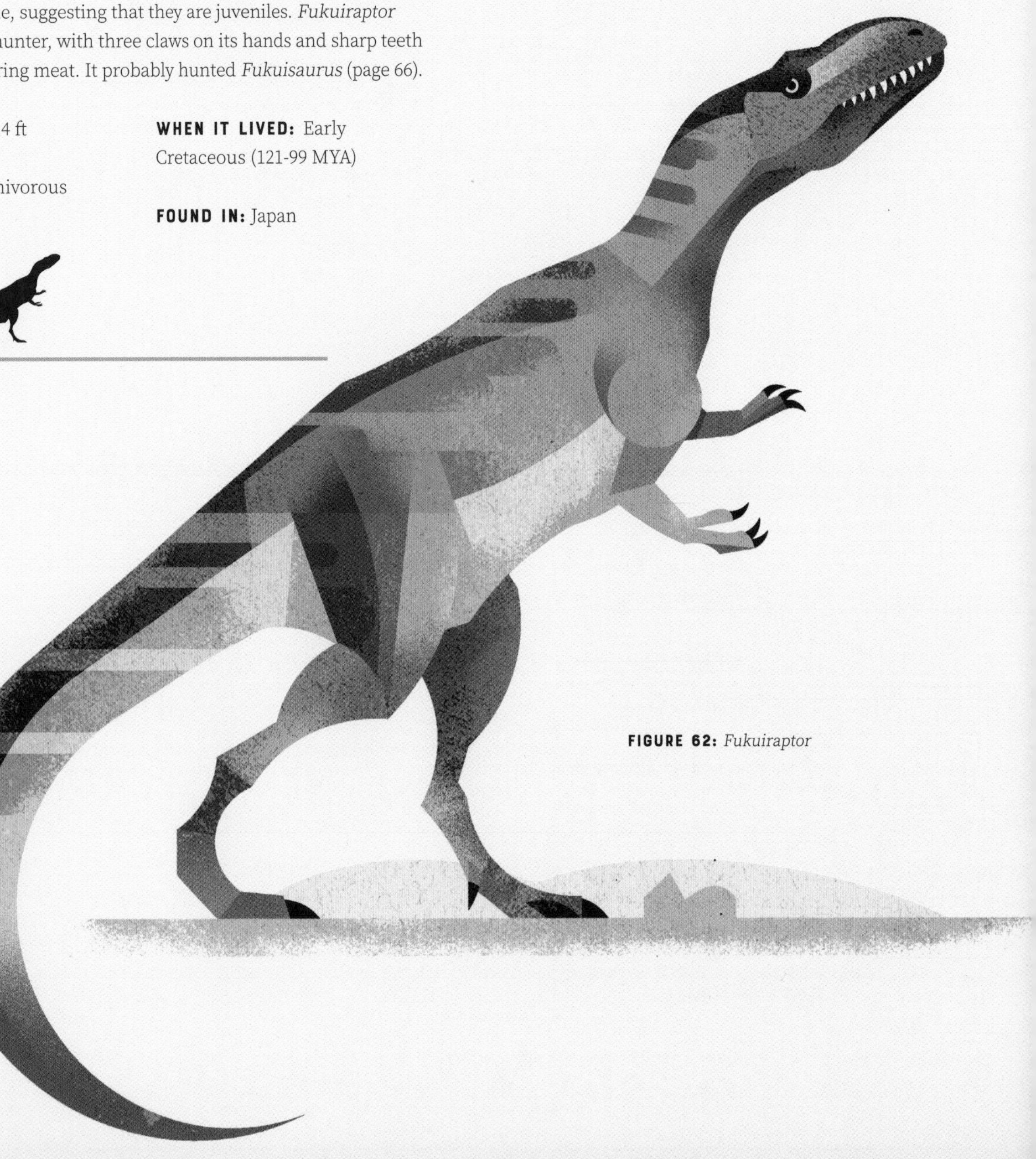

FIGURE 62: *Fukuiraptor*

G - L

GALLIMIMUS

(gal-eh-mime-us) **CHICKEN MIMIC**

Gallimimus was a member of a group of dinosaurs called the "bird-mimics"—which were named because they all stood on two legs and had beaks at the end of their skulls, just like modern birds. From what scientists know, *Gallimimus* was one of the largest members of the bird-mimic group. In life it could have grown up to twice the height of an adult human, making it much taller than its North American cousin, *Ornithomimus* (page 116).

LENGTH: 20 ft

DIET: Omnivorous

WHEN IT LIVED: Late Cretaceous (74-70 MYA)

FOUND IN: Mongolia

FIGURE 63: *Gallimimus*

GARGOYLEOSAURUS

(gahr-goy-lee-oh-sore-us) **GARGOYLE LIZARD**

LENGTH: 13 ft

DIET: Herbivorous

WHEN IT LIVED: Late Jurassic (154-142 MYA)

FOUND IN: USA

GASOSAURUS

(gas-oh-SORE-us) **GAS LIZARD**

Gasosaurus was a medium-sized meat-eater, but could have still weighed up to 882 pounds—heavier than four grown humans. *Gasosaurus* had three fingers on its hands, unlike bigger dinosaurs such as *Tyrannosaurus* (page 169), which only had two. It was also younger than *Tyrannosaurus* because it lived in the Jurassic Period, in what is now China.

LENGTH: 13 ft

WHEN IT LIVED: Mid Jurassic (170-160 MYA)

DIET: Carnivorous

FOUND IN: People's Republic of China

GARUDIMIMUS

(ga-roo-dee-mime-us) **GARUDA MIMIC**

LENGTH: 15 ft

WHEN IT LIVED: Late Cretaceous (99-89 MYA)

DIET: Omnivorous

FOUND IN: Mongolia

FIGURE 64: *Gasosaurus*

A B C D E F G H I J K L M N O P Q R S T U V W X Y Z

GASPARINISAURA

(gas-pah-reen-ee-sore-ra) **GASPARINI'S LIZARD**

LENGTH: About 2.5 ft

DIET: Herbivorous

WHEN IT LIVED: Late Cretaceous (86-71 MYA)

FOUND IN: Argentina

GASTONIA

(gas-toh-nee-ah) **[ROBERT] GASTON**

Gastonia was a beautiful, spiky, heavily-armored ankylosaur. Because of its 2-ton weight, it could only move very, very slowly on four legs. High plates projected from its sides and from its back, presumably to ward off predators, and possibly also as a form of display to other dinosaurs.

LENGTH: 15 ft

DIET: Herbivorous

WHEN IT LIVED: Early Cretaceous (142-127 MYA)

FOUND IN: USA

FIGURE 65: *Gastonia*

GIGANOTOSAURUS

(gig-an-OH-toe-SORE-us) **GIANT SOUTHERN LIZARD**

All the information we have about *Giganotosaurus* is based on what we can tell from very incomplete fossils. Although in pictures today it looks similar to *Tyrannosaurus* (page 169), we know that it was taller and longer—but slimmer. It lived millions of years earlier than *Tyrannosaurus* and would have roamed the plains of South America instead of North America. We also know that *Giganotosaurus* had three fingers on its hands, unlike *Tyrannosaurus's* two fingers.

LENGTH: 41 ft

DIET: Carnivorous

WHEN IT LIVED: Early Cretaceous (112-90 MYA)

FOUND IN: Argentina

FIGURE 66: *Giganotosaurus*

A
B
C
D
E
F
G
H
I
J
K
L
M
N
O
P
Q
R
S
T
U
V
W
X
Y
Z

FIGURE 67: *Gilmoreosaurus*

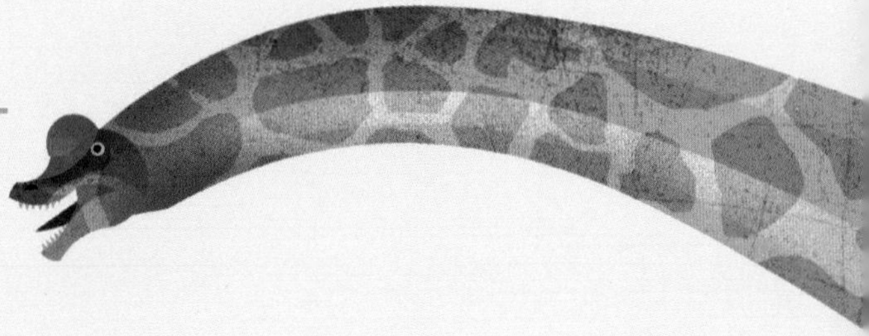

GILMOREOSAURUS

(GIL-more-oh-SORE-us) **GILMORE'S LIZARD**

This large herbivore was closely related to dinosaurs like *Iguanodon* (page 83) from the UK. It had a very long skull that ended in a beak, which would have been covered in a material called "keratin." It only ate plants, by grinding them down with its teeth, but it may have been hunted by large tyrannosaurs like *Alioramus* (page 13).

LENGTH: 20 ft

DIET: Herbivorous

WHEN IT LIVED:
Late Cretaceous (76-70 MYA)

FOUND IN: People's
Republic of China

GIRAFFATITAN

(ji-raf-a-tie-tan) **GIRAFFE TITAN**

Giraffatitan was first thought to be a type of African species of *Brachiosaurus* (page 33), but scientists later worked out that it was probably a completely different creature altogether, and so named it *Giraffatitan*. However, it would have had a very similar lifestyle to *Brachiosaurus*, spending its days browsing the trees for foliage to eat. Some think that it could have weighed a huge 77 tons.

LENGTH: 75 ft

DIET: Herbivorous

WHEN IT LIVED: Late Jurassic (154-142 MYA)

FOUND IN: Tanzania

GOBISAURUS

(goh-bee-sore-us) **GOBI LIZARD**

LENGTH: Up to 16 ft

DIET: Herbivorous

WHEN IT LIVED: Early Cretaceous (121-99 MYA)

FOUND IN: People's Republic of China

GORGOSAURUS

(gor-goh-sore-us) **FIERCE LIZARD**

LENGTH: 28 ft

DIET: Carnivorous

WHEN IT LIVED: Late Cretaceous (80-73 MYA)

FOUND IN: Canada and USA

FIGURE 68: *Giraffatitan*

A
B
C
D
E
F
G
H
I
J
K
L
M
N
O
P
Q
R
S
T
U
V
W
X
Y
Z

FIGURE 69: *Goyocephale*

GOYOCEPHALE

(goy-oh-keff-ah-lee) **DECORATED HEAD**

Goyocephale was a pachycephalosaur (a dinosaur with a thick, ridged skull). It only ate plants and would have run on two legs. On top of its head was an extra bone that formed a bumpy area, but unlike most pachycephalosaurs, it was not shaped into a high dome. The very top of its head did still have some small ridges on it, though, and these help scientists tell that it was still a member of the pachycephalosaur family.

LENGTH: 6.5 ft

DIET: Herbivorous

WHEN IT LIVED: Late Cretaceous (81-75 MYA)

FOUND IN: Mongolia

GRACILICERATOPS

(gras-i-li-serra-tops) **GRACILE HORNED FACE**

Graciliceratops was a tiny member of the ceratopsian group of dinosaurs—it may have only been 31 inches long. Although ceratopsians are known for their bony frills, *Graciliceratops* only had a small one. It had probably not yet evolved to be like the very large, ornamental ones seen in such dinosaurs as *Triceratops* (page 165)—which lived millions of years later.

LENGTH: 2.5-3 ft

WHEN IT LIVED: Late Cretaceous (99-84 MYA)

DIET: Herbivorous

FOUND IN: Mongolia

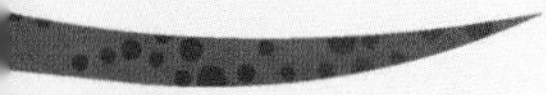

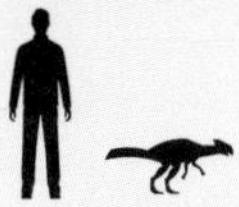

GRYPOSAURUS

(grip-oh-sore-us) **HOOK-NOSED LIZARD**

LENGTH: 32 ft

WHEN IT LIVED: Late Cretaceous (86-71 MYA)

DIET: Herbivorous

FOUND IN: Canada and USA

GUAIBASAURUS

(gwie-bah-sore-us) **RIO GUAIBA LIZARD**

LENGTH: About 6 ft

WHEN IT LIVED: Late Triassic (221-210 MYA)

DIET: Herbivorous

FOUND IN: Brazil

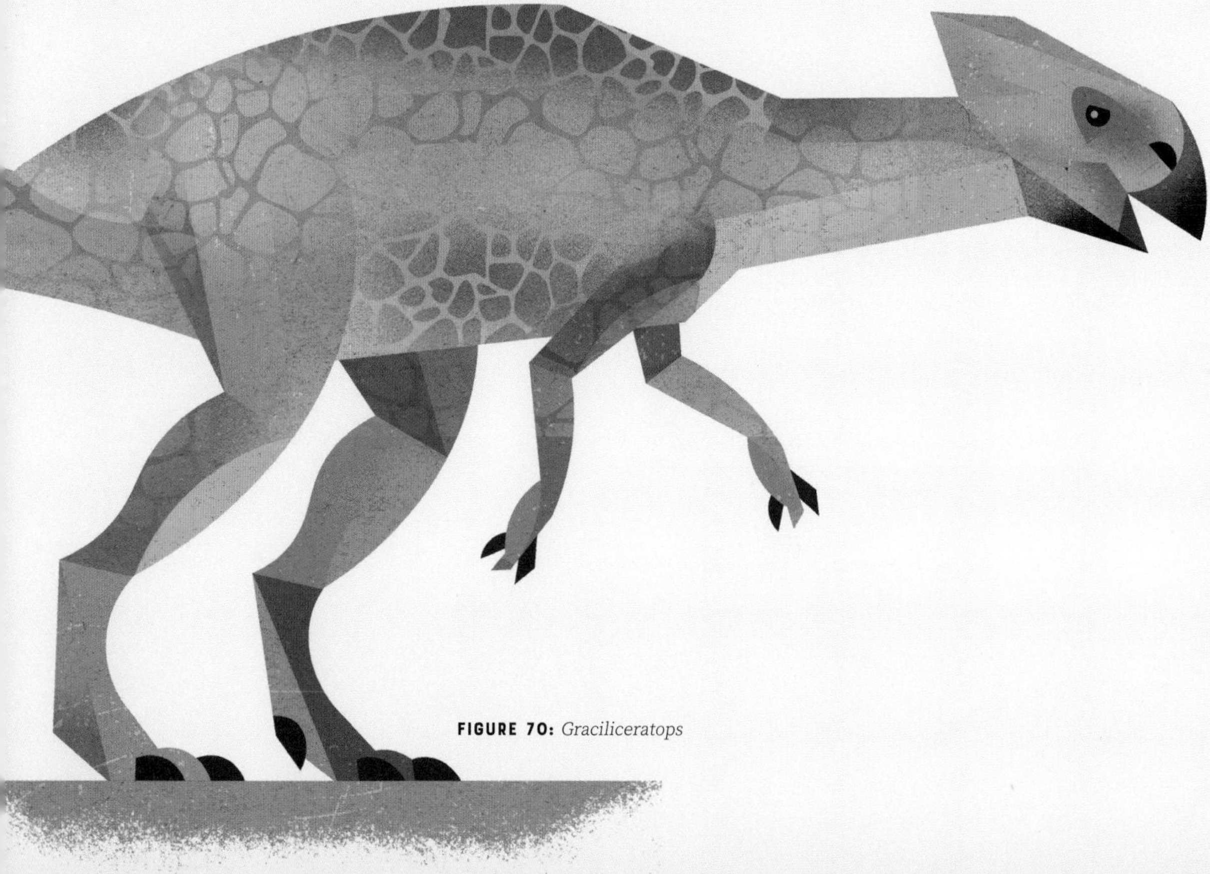

FIGURE 70: *Graciliceratops*

GUANLONG

(gwan-long) **CROWNED DRAGON**

LENGTH: 10 ft

DIET: Carnivorous

WHEN IT LIVED: Late Jurassic (159-154 MYA)

FOUND IN: People's Republic of China

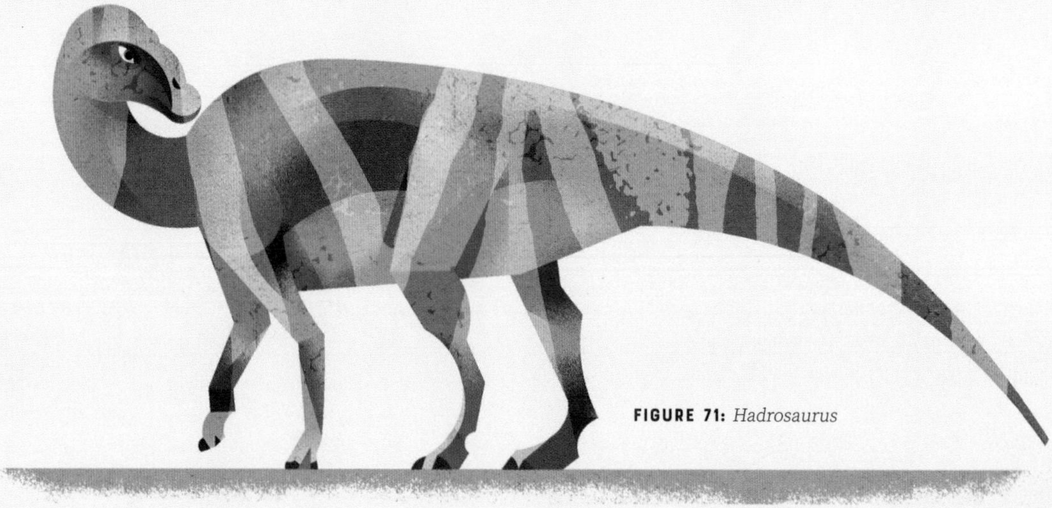

FIGURE 71: *Hadrosaurus*

HADROSAURUS

(HAD-row-SORE-us) **BIG LIZARD**

Hadrosaurus was a large, two-legged herbivore from the hadrosaur group of dinosaurs, which would have cropped vegetation with its beak. Its name means "bulky lizard" because it was so large and so heavy, and was the first hadrosaur ever named. It may have been hunted by large tyrannosaurs, but giant crocodiles would have also been a danger in Cretaceous North America.

LENGTH: 30 ft

DIET: Herbivorous

WHEN IT LIVED: Late Cretaceous (78-74 MYA)

FOUND IN: USA

HAGRYPHUS

(ha-grif-us) **HA (EGYPTIAN GOD OF THE WESTERN DESERT)**

The only fossils scientists have of *Hagryphus* are of its left hand and some parts of the foot and toes. Most of what we know is actually based on reconstructions of *Chirostenotes* (page 45)—a very similar dinosaur. From comparing them with one another, we know that *Hagryphus* must have had feathers and a short beak at the end of its snout. It probably also walked on two legs and could run very quickly.

LENGTH: 10 ft

DIET: Omnivorous

WHEN IT LIVED: Late Cretaceous (75 MYA)

FOUND IN: USA

HAPLOCANTHOSAURUS

(hap-lo-kan-tho-sore-us) **SIMPLE-SPINED LIZARD**

LENGTH: Up to 71 ft

DIET: Herbivorous

WHEN IT LIVED: Late Jurassic (154-142 MYA)

FOUND IN: USA

FIGURE 72: *Hagryphus*

A
B
C
D
E
F
G
H
I
J
K
L
M
N
O
P
Q
R
S
T
U
V
W
X
Y
Z

HARPYMIMUS

(harp-pee-mime-us) **HARPY MIMIC**

LENGTH: 6.5 ft

DIET: Omnivorous

WHEN IT LIVED: Early Cretaceous (121-99 MYA)

FOUND IN: Mongolia

HERRERASAURUS

(herr-ray-rah-SORE-us) **HERRERA'S LIZARD**

LENGTH: 10 ft

DIET: Carnivorous

WHEN IT LIVED: Late Triassic (228 MYA)

FOUND IN: Argentina

HESPEROSAURUS

(hes-per-oh-sore-us) **WESTERN LIZARD**

Hesperosaurus was a stegosaur, like *Stegosaurus* (page 153). It had plates running along its back, but they would have been wide and short—instead of tall like *Stegosaurus*'s plates. We do not know for certain what these plates were used for, but they may have been useful for telling different species apart. *Hesperosaurus* had spikes on the end of its tail, which it used as a defensive weapon, called a "thagomizer."

LENGTH: 20 ft

DIET: Herbivorous

WHEN IT LIVED: Late Jurassic (154-142 MYA)

FOUND IN: USA

FIGURE 73: *Hesperosaurus*

FIGURE 74: *Heterodontosaurus*

HETERODONTOSAURUS

(HET-er-oh-DON'T-oh-sore-us)

DIFFERENT-TEETH LIZARD

Heterodontosaurus was a small and speedy herbivore. It had sharp, tusk-like teeth in the front of its mouth and flat, plant-grinding teeth in the back. The bone structure of *Heterodontosaurus* is strange because it looks a lot like some meat-eating dinosaurs. The claws on its hands and feet were curved and sharp, and some scientists think that they may have been used to dig up the ground to find food.

LENGTH: 4 ft

DIET: Herbivorous

WHEN IT LIVED: Early Jurassic (200-190 MYA)

FOUND IN: Lesotho and South Africa

HOMALOCEPHALE

(home-ah-loh-keff-ah-lee) **LEVEL HEAD**

LENGTH: 5 ft

DIET: Herbivorous

WHEN IT LIVED: Late Cretaceous (72-68 MYA)

FOUND IN: Mongolia

HUAYANGOSAURUS

(hoy-YANG-oh-SORE-us) **HUAYANG LIZARD**

Huayangosaurus was one of the earliest members of the stegosaur group of dinosaurs. Instead of big plates on its back—like *Stegosaurus* (page 153) would have had—this dinosaur had smaller, thinner spines, as well as a large spine on each shoulder. Scientists are not sure if these were for defending itself from predators or for displaying to other dinosaurs.

LENGTH: 15 ft

DIET: Herbivorous

WHEN IT LIVED: Mid Jurassic (170-160 MYA)

FOUND IN: People's Republic of China

HYLAEOSAURUS

(HIGH-lee-oh-sore-us) **WOODLAND LIZARD**

Hylaeosaurus was one of the first three fossils ever identified as a "dinosaur" by Richard Owen in 1841. Although it was an ankylosaur (armored dinosaur), it lacked a large and heavy tail club. Its place in the dinosaur family tree is a bit of a mystery, and scientists today cannot agree if it is more closely related to *Ankylosaurus* (page 18), *Nodosaurus* (page 113), or *Polacanthus* (page 129).

LENGTH: 16 ft

DIET: Herbivorous

WHEN IT LIVED: Early Cretaceous (150-135 MYA)

FOUND IN: England

HYPACROSAURUS

(hi-pak-roh-sore-us) **NEAR-TOPMOST LIZARD**

LENGTH: 30 ft

DIET: Herbivorous

WHEN IT LIVED: Late Cretaceous (70 MYA)

FOUND IN: Canada and USA

FIGURE 75: *Huayangosaurus*

FIGURE 76: *Hylaeosaurus*

HYPSELOSAURUS

(hip-sel-O-saw-rus) **HIGHEST LIZARD**

Fossils of *Hypselosaurus* were first found in France in the late 1800s. Its name means "highest lizard" because of how high its neck was thought to be able to reach when searching tree tops for leaves to eat. Fossils of two raptors were also found in the same layers of rock as *Hypselosaurus*, which may show that they hunted *Hypselosaurus*.

LENGTH: 50 ft

DIET: Herbivorous

WHEN IT LIVED: Late Cretaceous (70 MYA)

FOUND IN: France

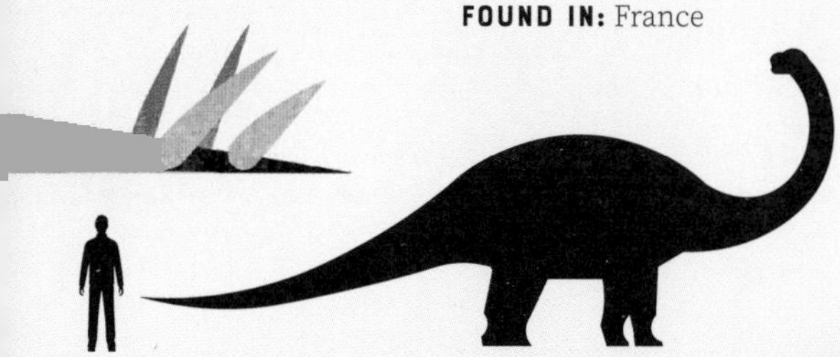

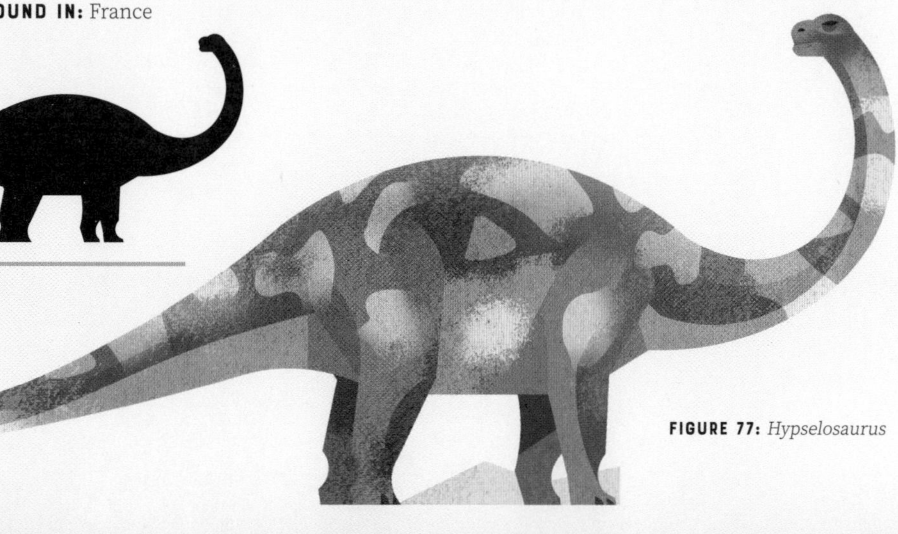

FIGURE 77: *Hypselosaurus*

HYPSELOSPINUS

(hip-sell-o-spine-us) **HIGH SPINED**

LENGTH: About 20 ft

DIET: Herbivore

WHEN IT LIVED: Early Cretaceous, Valangian (141-137 MYA)

FOUND IN: England

HYPSILOPHODON

(hip-sih-LOH-foh-don) **HIGH-RIDGE TOOTH**

So far, no adult fossils of *Hypsilophodon* have been found—only juveniles, which seems very odd to scientists. This small dinosaur lived in the UK in the Cretaceous Period, and would only have eaten plants. It was once suggested that *Hypsilophodon* lived in trees, but this idea is no longer accepted by scientists.

LENGTH: 7.5 ft

DIET: Herbivorous

WHEN IT LIVED: Early Cretaceous (125 MYA)

FOUND IN: England and Spain

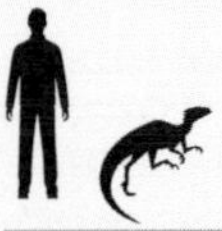

FIGURE 78: *Hypsilophodon*

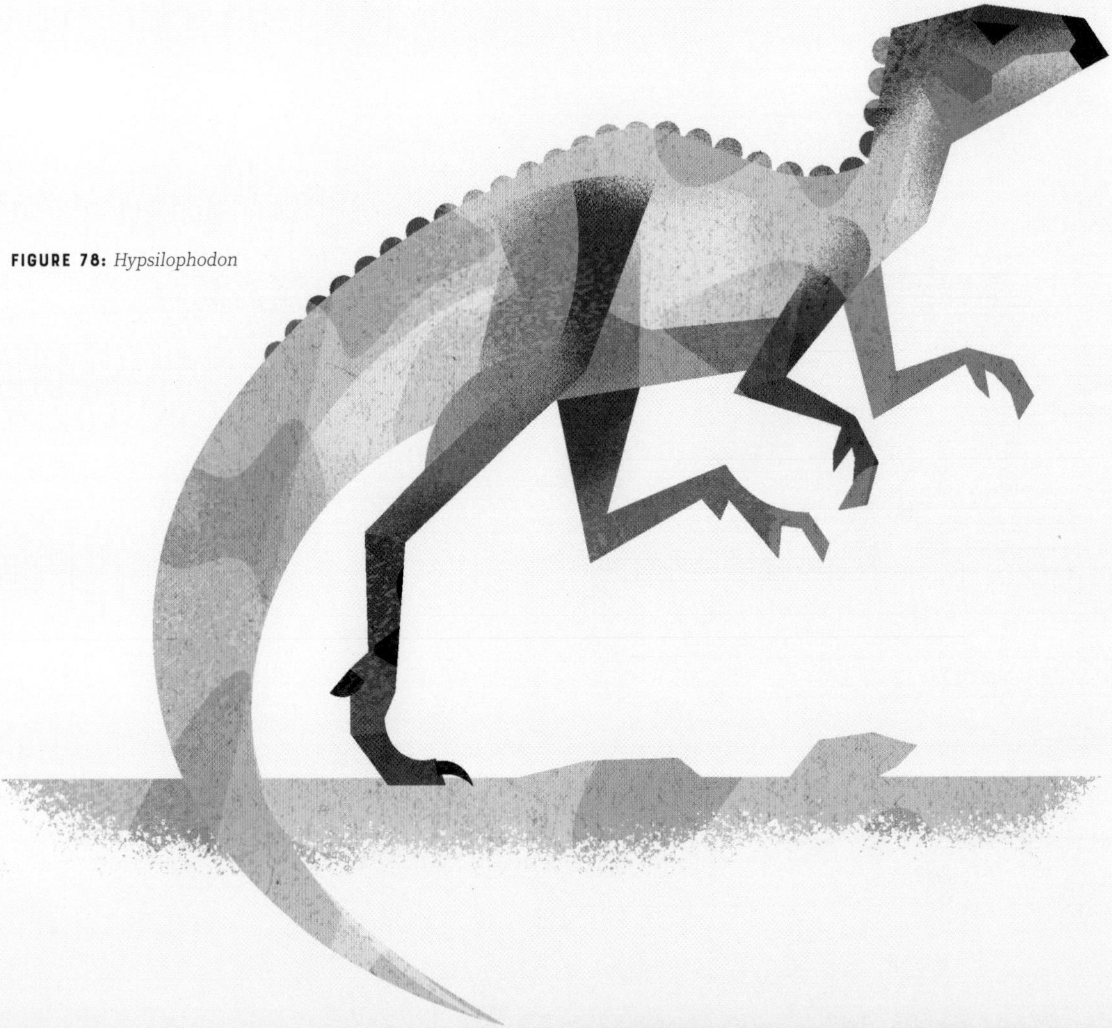

IGUANODON

(ig-WHA-noh-don) **IGUANA TOOTH**

Iguanodon could probably choose to either walk on all four legs or on just two legs. It is thought to have been one of the most successful dinosaurs because its remains have been found in many parts of the world. It had a large thumb spike on the end of its hand, probably to fend off predators, and the structure of the muscles inside its head suggest it had a very long tongue.

LENGTH: 32 ft

DIET: Herbivorous

WHEN IT LIVED: Early Cretaceous (140-110 MYA)

FOUND IN: England, Germany, USA, Spain, and Belgium

FIGURE 79: *Iguanodon*

FIGURE 80: *Indosuchus*

INDOSUCHUS

(in-doh-sook-us) **INDIAN CROCODILE**

An almost-complete skeleton of *Indosuchus* has been found. It was a large abelisaurid dinosaur—which means that it was a two-legged meat-eater with very short arms but a deep and powerful snout for biting prey. It had sharp teeth that could easily rip through flesh, which it probably relied on to bite and subdue it prey.

LENGTH: 23 ft

DIET: Carnivorous

WHEN IT LIVED: Late Cretaceous (71-65 MYA)

FOUND IN: India

INGENIA

(ing-gay-nee-ah) **INGENI-KHOBUR**

LENGTH: 6.5 ft

DIET: Omnivorous

WHEN IT LIVED: Late Cretaceous (72-68 MYA)

FOUND IN: Mongolia

IRRITATOR

(irr-it-ate-or) **IRRITATOR**

LENGTH: 21 ft

DIET: Carnivorous

WHEN IT LIVED: Early Cretaceous (112-100 MYA)

FOUND IN: Brazil

ISISAURUS

(iss-ee-sore-us) **ISI (INDIAN STATISTICAL INSTITUTE) LIZARD**

Isisaurus was one of the larger dinosaurs that roamed around what is now India, during the Cretaceous Period. As a titanosaur, it would have been a huge long-necked and long-tailed sauropod that browsed high trees for leaves. Fossilized poop from this dinosaur shows that it ate from a wide variety of trees.

LENGTH: Up to 60 ft

DIET: Herbivorous

WHEN IT LIVED: Late Cretaceous (71-65 MYA)

FOUND IN: India

FIGURE 81: *Isisaurus*

A
B
C
D
E
F
G
H
I
J
K
L
M
N
O
P
Q
R
S
T
U
V
W
X
Y
Z

JANENSCHIA

(yan-ensh-ee-ah) **NAMED AFTER JANENSCH**

Janenschia was a large sauropod from Tanzania in East Africa. It had a very long neck for reaching up to high trees, and it walked on all four legs. *Janenschia's* tail also would have been very long. We know all of this mostly from comparing its fossils to the fossils of other, similar sauropods.

LENGTH: 65 ft

DIET: Herbivorous

WHEN IT LIVED: Late Jurassic (154-151 MYA)

FOUND IN: Tanzania

FIGURE 82: *Janenschia*

JAXARTOSAURUS

(jak-sahr-toh-sore-us) **JAXARTES [RIVER] LIZARD**

LENGTH: 30 ft

DIET: Herbivorous

WHEN IT LIVED: Late Cretaceous (94-84 MYA)

FOUND IN: Kazakhstan

FIGURE 83: *Jinzhousaurus*

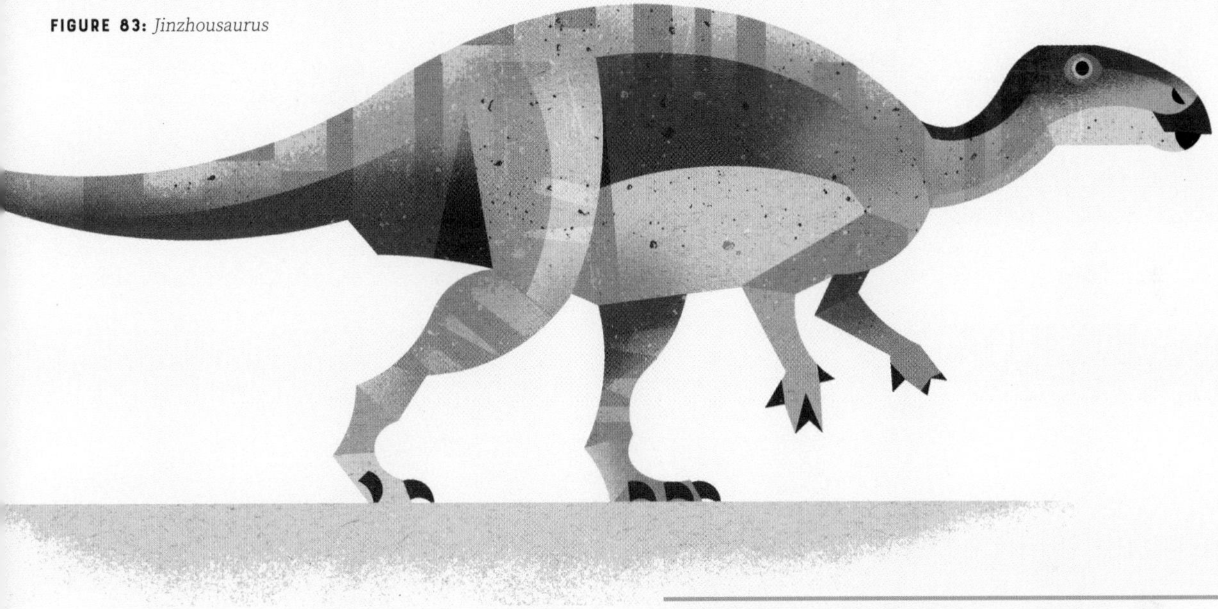

JINGSHANOSAURUS

(jing-shahn-oh-sore-us) **JINGSHAN LIZARD**

LENGTH: 16 ft

DIET: Herbivorous

WHEN IT LIVED: Early Jurassic (205-190 MYA)

FOUND IN: People's Republic of China

JINZHOUSAURUS

(jeen-joh-sore-us) **JINZHOU LIZARD**

Jinzhousaurus was a herbivore that grazed on low vegetation. Scientists still cannot decide if it belongs in the same group as *Iguanodon* (page 83) or *Hadrosaurus* (page 76). Usefully, the fossils that are known to scientists are almost complete and all the bones have been found together in the positions they would have been in life. Scientists call this being "fully articulated."

LENGTH: 23 ft

DIET: Herbivorous

WHEN IT LIVED: Early Cretaceous (127-121 MYA)

FOUND IN: People's Republic of China

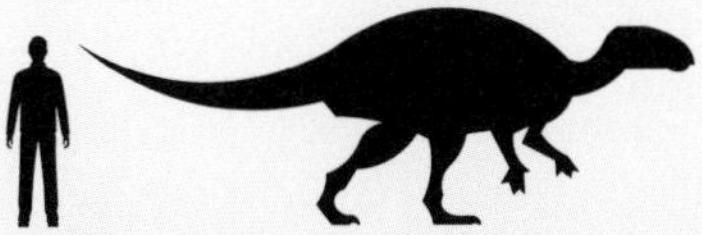

JOBARIA

(joh-bahr-ee-uh) **JOBAR (MYTHICAL ANIMAL)**

Jobaria was a sauropod from Niger in Africa, and is named after a large, mythological beast from that country, called Jobar. Over 90% of its skeleton is known, making it one of the most complete species of sauropods. This means that *Jobaria* can offer scientists lots of important information about the lifestyle of these long-necked animals.

LENGTH: 70 ft

DIET: Herbivorous

WHEN IT LIVED: Middle Jurassic (132-94 MYA)

FOUND IN: Niger

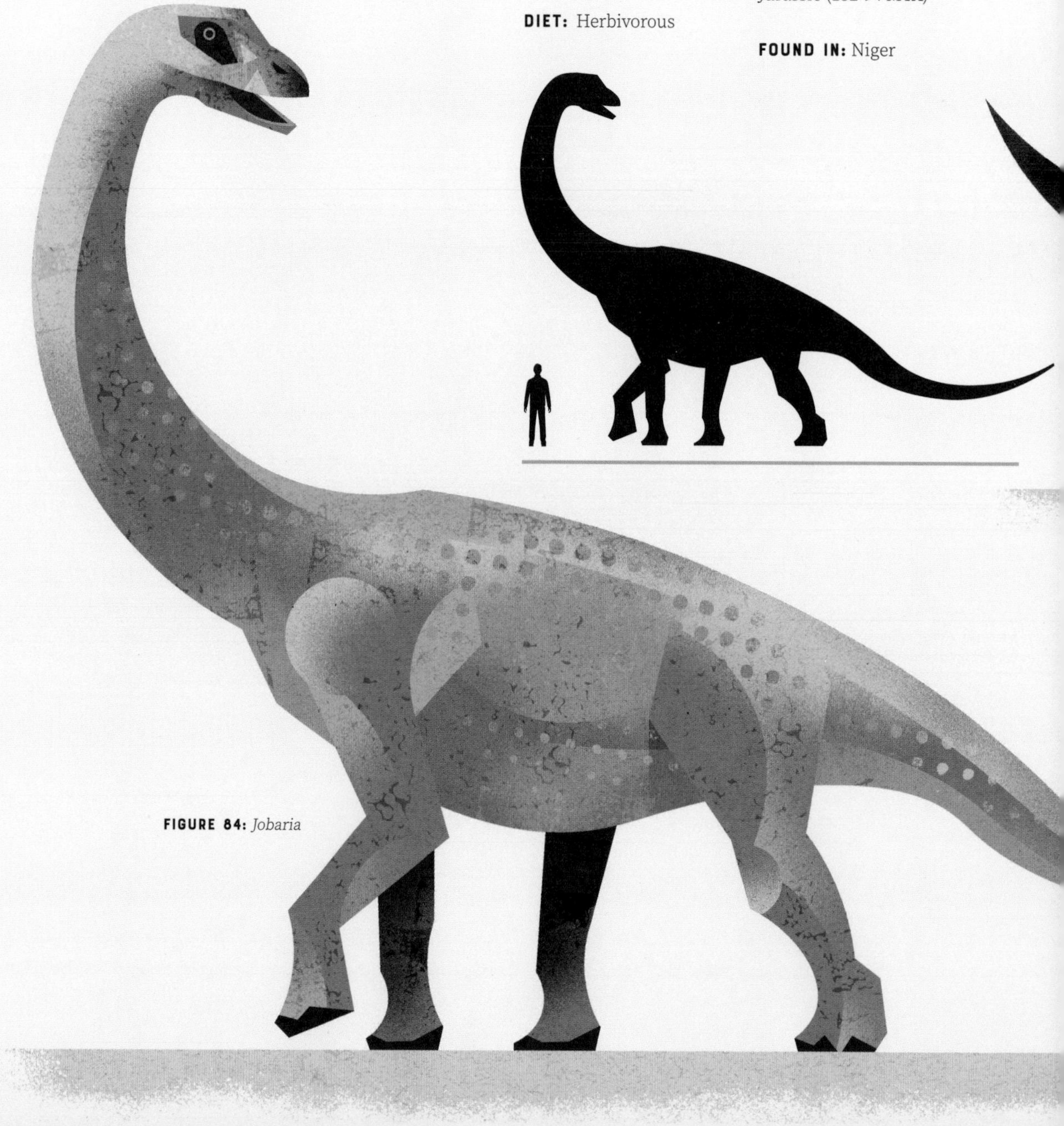

FIGURE 84: *Jobaria*

K

KENTROSAURUS

(ken-TROH-sore-us) **SPIKY LIZARD**

LENGTH: 16 ft

WHEN IT LIVED: Late Jurassic (155-150 MYA)

DIET: Herbivorous

FOUND IN: Tanzania

L

LAMACERATOPS

(lah-mah-serra-tops) **LAMA (BUDDHIST MONK) HORNED FACE**

LENGTH: 3-6.5 ft

WHEN IT LIVED: Late Cretaceous (75-72 MYA)

DIET: Herbivorous

FOUND IN: Mongolia

FIGURE 85: *Lambeosaurus*

LAMBEOSAURUS

(lam-BEE-oh-SORE-us) **LAMBE'S LIZARD**

Lambeosaurus had a bony crest that projected upward from the top of its head. This crest, which was for display and signaling to other dinosaurs, may have been flushed with blood so that it changed color. It is possible that male and females of this species of dinosaur had different sized or shaped crests. Despite being huge in size, *Lambeosaurus* would only have eaten plants to fuel its enormous body.

LENGTH: 30 ft

WHEN IT LIVED: Late Cretaceous (76-74 MYA)

DIET: Herbivorous

FOUND IN: Canada

A B C D E F G H I J K L M N O P Q R S T U V W X Y Z

LAPPARENTOSAURUS

(la-pah-rent-oh-sore-us) **LAPPARENT'S LIZARD**

LENGTH: Up to 50 ft

DIET: Herbivorous

WHEN IT LIVED: Mid Jurassic (169-164 MYA)

FOUND IN: Madagascar

FIGURE 86: *Leptoceratops*

LEAELLYNASAURA

(LEE-ELL-IN-a-SORE-a) **LEAELLYN'S LIZARD**

LENGTH: 6.5 ft

DIET: Herbivorous

WHEN IT LIVED: Early Cretaceous (115-110 MYA)

FOUND IN: Australia

LEPTOCERATOPS

(lep-toh-ker-ah-tops) **SLIM HORNED FACE**

Leptoceratops was only very small—about the size of a small dog today. However, we know that this dinosaur and its close relatives would eventually have evolved to give rise to the group of dinosaurs that includes the giant *Triceratops* (page 165) and *Styracosaurus* (page 156). Like these later dinosaurs, *Leptoceratops* probably only ate plants, but unlike them, it could run on two legs instead of four.

LENGTH: 10 ft

DIET: Herbivorous

WHEN IT LIVED: Late Cretaceous (67-65 MYA)

FOUND IN: Canada and USA

LESOTHOSAURUS

(leh-su-too-sore-us) **LESOTHO LIZARD**

Lesothosaurus was a small ornithischian (dinosaurs with hip bones like a birds') and was probably no bigger than a house cat. Some scientists think that it lived in burrows for safety, and we now know that it traveled in family groups. This dinosaur had five fingers on each "hand," although these were probably not very good at grasping.

LENGTH: 3 ft

DIET: Herbivorous

WHEN IT LIVED: Early Jurassic (200-190 MYA)

FOUND IN: Lesotho

FIGURE 87: *Lesothosaurus*

LEXOVISAURUS

(lex-oh-vee-sore-us) **LEXOVII LIZARD**

LENGTH: 16-20 ft

DIET: Herbivorous

WHEN IT LIVED: Late Jurassic (170-150 MYA)

FOUND IN: England, France

LIAOCERATOPS

(lee-ow-serra-tops) **LIAONING HORNED FACE**

Liaoceratops was a small herbivore belonging to the group of horned and bony frilled dinosaurs called the ceratopsians. But *Liaoceratops* was one of the earliest ceratopsians in the family tree, so it had not yet developed the elaborate neck frill seen in later ceratopsians like *Triceratops* (page 165). Instead, it would have looked much more like the parrot-beaked *Psittacosaurus* (page 134), and may have also had bristles sticking out of its back.

LENGTH: 3-6.5 ft

DIET: Herbivorous

WHEN IT LIVED: Early Cretaceous (127-121 MYA)

FOUND IN: People's Republic of China

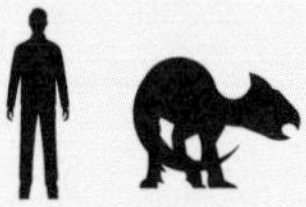

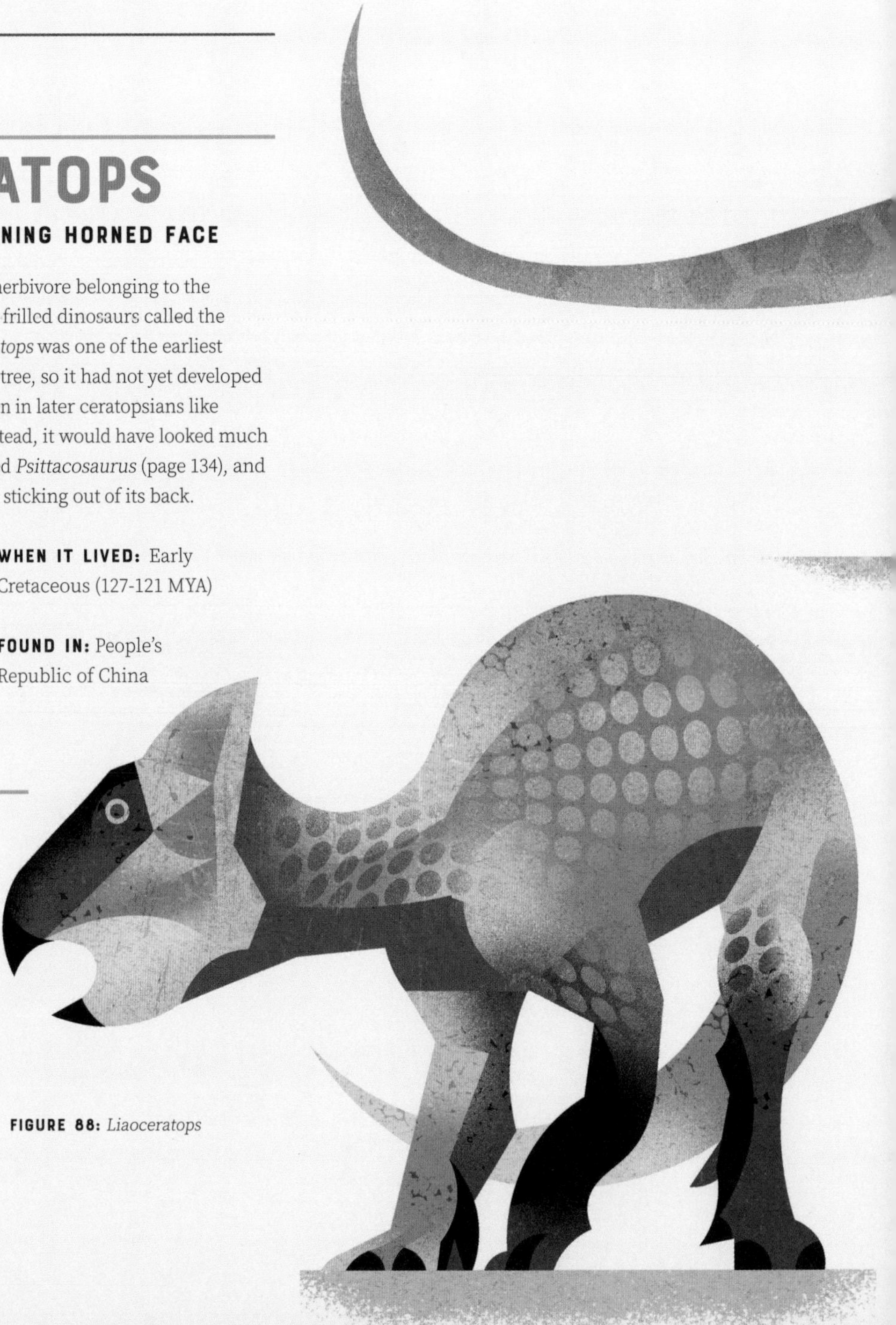

FIGURE 88: *Liaoceratops*

FIGURE 89: *Ligabuesaurus*

LIAOXIORNIS

(lyow-shee-or-nis) **LIAOXI BIRD**

LENGTH: About 3 in

DIET: Carnivorous

WHEN IT LIVED: Early Cretaceous (127-121 MYA)

FOUND IN: People's Republic of China

LIGABUESAURUS

(lee-gah-boo-sore-us) **[DR GIANCARLO] LIGABUE LIZARD**

Although *Ligabuesaurus* is only known from a few fragments of fossils, scientists can piece together the skeleton of this giant herbivore by comparing it with other close relatives. We know that it must have been a long-necked tree browser and that it probably walked on all four legs.

LENGTH: 78 ft

DIET: Herbivorous

WHEN IT LIVED: Early Cretaceous (121-99 MYA)

FOUND IN: Argentina

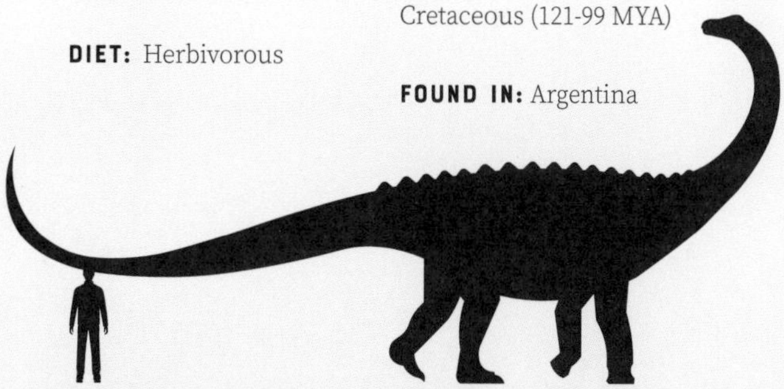

LILIENSTERNUS

(lil-ee-en-shtern-us) **FOR LILIENSTERN**

One of the earliest predators, *Liliensternus* was a swift and agile hunter. Scientists know from looking at the fossils of this dinosaur that it had very good eyesight. Its arms were shorter than its neck, meaning that it could not use its hands to grasp its prey while it ate—so it must have just used its head when feeding. It probably hunted early sauropod relatives, but also some smaller theropods like *Coelophysis* (page 46).

LENGTH: 16 ft

DIET: Carnivorous

WHEN IT LIVED: Late Triassic (205-202 MYA)

FOUND IN: Germany and France

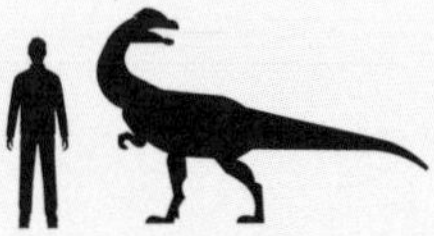

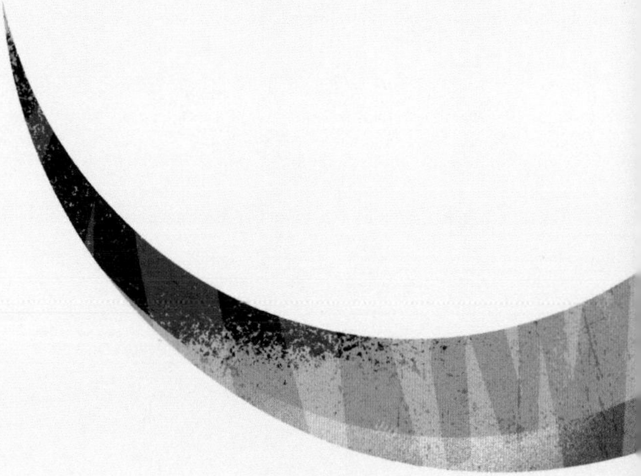

LOPHORHOTHON

(lof-oh-roh-thon) **CRESTED NOSE**

LENGTH: About 15 ft

DIET: Herbivorous

WHEN IT LIVED: Late Cretaceous (84-71 MYA)

FOUND IN: USA

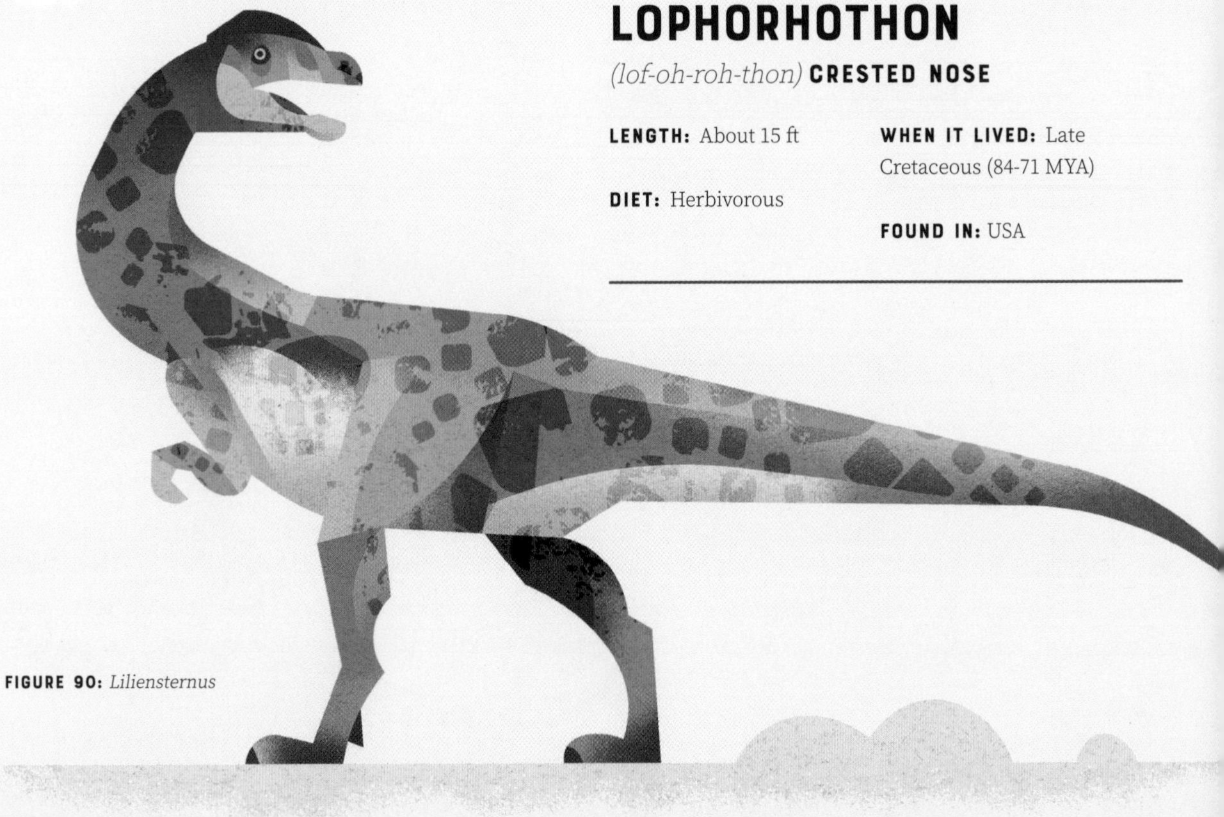

FIGURE 90: *Liliensternus*

FIGURE 91: *Lufengosaurus*

LUFENGOSAURUS

(loo-FUNG-oh-SORE-us) **LUFENG LIZARD**

Lufengosaurus was a plant-eating dinosaur in the group that contained other big dinosaurs like *Diplodocus* (page 55) and *Apatosaurus* (page 20). However, *Lufengosaurus* was smaller than these, and could walk on two legs instead of four. It probably stood up on two legs while it used its long neck to reach for high branches, and its hands might have held the trunk of the tree for support.

LENGTH: 20 ft

DIET: Herbivorous

WHEN IT LIVED: Early Jurassic (200-195 MYA)

FOUND IN: People's Republic of China

LOPHOSTROPHEUS

(lof-oh-stro-fee-us) **CRESTED VEREBRA**

LENGTH: 20 ft

DIET: Carnivorous

WHEN IT LIVED: Early Jurassic (203-196 MYA)

FOUND IN: France

LURDUSAURUS
(loor-duh-sore-us) **HEAVY LIZARD**

Lurdusaurus was a large hadrosaur dinosaur, like *Hadrosaurus* (page 76), and its size is what led to scientists deciding to call it the "heavy lizard." It certainly could not run very fast, and may have had to live in herds as a way of protecting itself from predators.

LENGTH: 30 ft

DIET: Herbivorous

WHEN IT LIVED: Early Cretaceous (121-112 MYA)

FOUND IN: Niger

LYCORHINUS
(liek-oh-rien-us) **WOLF SNOUT**

LENGTH: 4 ft

DIET: Herbivorous

WHEN IT LIVED: Late Triassic (205-195 MYA)

FOUND IN: South Africa

FIGURE 92: *Lurdusaurus*

M

FIGURE 93: *Maiasaura*

FIGURE 93: *Maiasaura*

MAGYAROSAURUS

(lmod-yar-oh-sore-us) **MAGYAR LIZARD**

LENGTH: 16-20 ft

WHEN IT LIVED: Late Cretaceous (71-65 MYA)

DIET: Herbivorous

FOUND IN: Romania

MAIASAURA

(my-ah-SORE-ah) **GOOD MOTHER LIZARD**

Maiasaura was a hadrosaur that only ate plants. Its name means "good mother lizard" because fossils of this dinosaur have been found surrounding nests and eggs at a site called Egg Mountain, in the USA. This suggests that *Maiasaura* looked after its eggs. Its name ends in "saura" instead of "saurus" because this is the female version of a dinosaur name—and the first *Maiasaura* to be found was a female. In fact, *Maiasaura* was the first ever dinosaur to be given a female name.

LENGTH: 30 ft

WHEN IT LIVED: Late Cretaceous (80-75 MYA)

DIET: Herbivorous

FOUND IN: USA

MAJUNGASAURUS

(mah-joong-gah-thol-us) **MAJUNGA DOME**

Most scientists today use the name *Majungasaurus* instead of *Majungatholus* for this dinosaur. It was an abelisaurid—which were a group of dinosaurs with tiny arms but powerful legs and strong jaws. It probably hunted huge sauropods, also known as titanosaurs.

LENGTH: 20 ft

DIET: Carnivorous

WHEN IT LIVED: Late Cretaceous (84-71 MYA)

FOUND IN: Madagascar

MALAWISAURUS

(mah-lah-wee-sore-us) **MALAWI LIZARD**

LENGTH: 30 ft

DIET: Herbivorous

WHEN IT LIVED: Early Cretaceous (121-112 MYA)

FOUND IN: Malawi

FIGURE 94: *Majungasaurus*

MAMENCHISAURUS

(mah-men-chi-sore-us) **MAMENCHI LIZARD**

Mamenchisaurus was a giant, long-necked tree browser and had a heavy body that needed supporting on all four legs. *Mamenchisaurus*'s flexible neck would have allowed it to easily eat enough food from the treetops to fuel its huge size without needing to move too far.

LENGTH: 72 ft

DIET: Herbivorous

WHEN IT LIVED: Late Jurassic (155-145 MYA)

FOUND IN: People's Republic of China

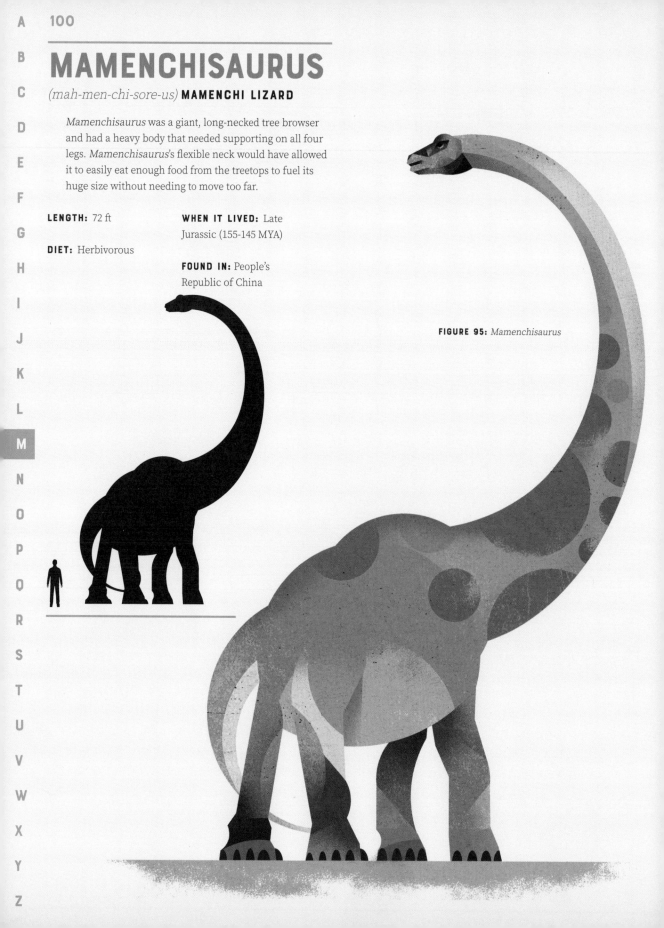

FIGURE 95: *Mamenchisaurus*

FIGURE 96: *Mapusaurus*

MAPUSAURUS

(mah-puh-sore-us) **EARTH LIZARD**

Mapusaurus would have been at the top of the food chain in its environment. It may have been even bigger than the mighty *Giganotosaurus* (page 71), making it the largest meat-eating dinosaur found so far. It probably grew to be over 39 feet in length, which is longer than six adult humans lying head-to-toe on the ground. Terrifyingly, the skull of *Mapusaurus* may have been almost as long as a human is tall. It probably hunted in packs and lived in family groups.

LENGTH: About 43 ft

DIET: Carnivorous

WHEN IT LIVED: Late Cretaceous (99-94 MYA)

FOUND IN: Argentina

MARSHOSAURUS

(marsh-oh-sore-us) **MARSH LIZARD**

LENGTH: 20 ft

DIET: Carnivorous

WHEN IT LIVED: Late Jurassic (154-142 MYA)

FOUND IN: USA

MASIAKASAURUS

(mah-shee-ah-kah-sore-us) **VICIOUS LIZARD**

LENGTH: 6.5 ft

DIET: Carnivorous

WHEN IT LIVED: Late Cretaceous (84-71 MYA)

FOUND IN: Madagascar

MASSOSPONDYLUS

(mass-oh-SPON-di-luss) **MASSIVE VERTEBRAE**

Massospondylus was one of the earliest long-necked tree browsers to walk the planet. It would have looked very different than the other dinosaurs in its group, like *Apatosaurus* (page 20), which came millions of years later. It was smaller than *Apatosaurus* and walked on two legs most of the time, instead of four. Many *Massospondylus* eggs were found in South Africa, and some contained baby dinosaurs that had not yet hatched, which scientists call "embryos."

LENGTH: 13 ft

DIET: Omnivorous

WHEN IT LIVED: Early Jurassic (200-190 MYA)

FOUND IN: Lesotho, South Africa, and Zimbabwe

FIGURE 97: *Massospondylus*

MAXAKALISAURUS

(max-aka-li-sore-us) **MAXAKALI (TRIBE OF BRAZIL) LIZARD**

Maxakalisaurus is one of the largest dinosaurs to have been found in Brazil. Like *Saltasaurus* (page 139), it had small, bony nodules in its skin which would have helped protect it from attack by other dinosaurs. Its diet would have been made up entirely of leaves, and its teeth formed a continuous row of pegs, like a comb, to scrape them off tree branches.

LENGTH: 43 ft

DIET: Herbivorous

WHEN IT LIVED: Late Cretaceous (80 MYA)

FOUND IN: Brazil

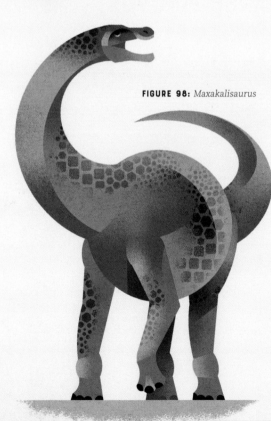

FIGURE 98: *Maxakalisaurus*

FIGURE 99: *Megalosaurus*

MEGALOSAURUS

(MEG-ah-low-sore-us) **BIG LIZARD**

Megalosaurus was one of the first dinosaur discoveries in
the world. It was also one of the first truly large predators
to walk the planet: it stalked the shores of the UK in the
Middle Jurassic Period, back when Britain was a series
of small tropical islands—like the Bahamas are today.
It would have fed upon many herbivores, including
stegosaurs and sauropods, as well as some of the marine
life that washed up on the coast.

LENGTH: 30 ft

WHEN IT LIVED: Mid
Jurassic (170-155 MYA)

DIET: Carnivorous

FOUND IN: England

MELANOROSAURUS

(me-lan-or-oh-sore-us) **BLACK MOUNTAIN LIZARD**

Melanorosaurus was one of the first sauropods to experiment with walking on four legs rather than two. We now know that sauropods evolved to be this way because their stomachs became too heavy to support on two legs alone, as their diets became filled with more and more plant matter. Once they became four-legged, they had little choice but to grow as big as they could. This is because four-legged walking would have been slower, and once they lost speed, size became their only defense against predators.

LENGTH: 40 ft

WHEN IT LIVED: Late Triassic (227-221 MYA)

DIET: Omnivorous

FOUND IN: South Africa

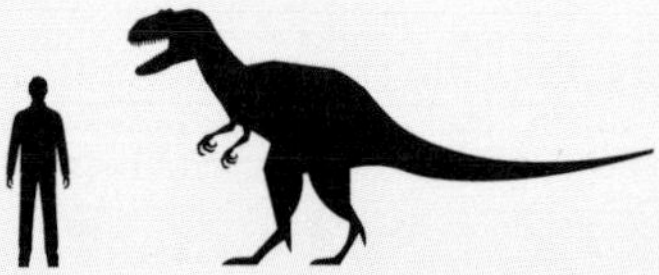

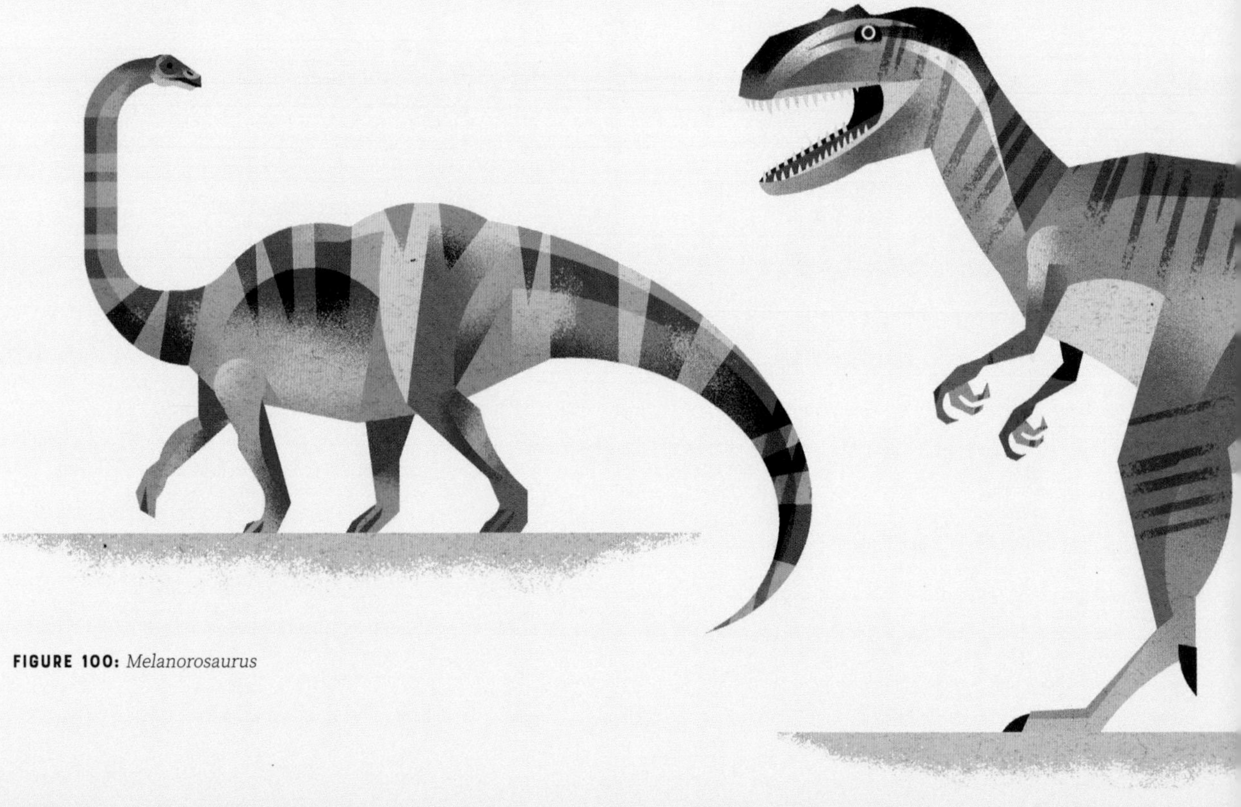

FIGURE 100: *Melanorosaurus*

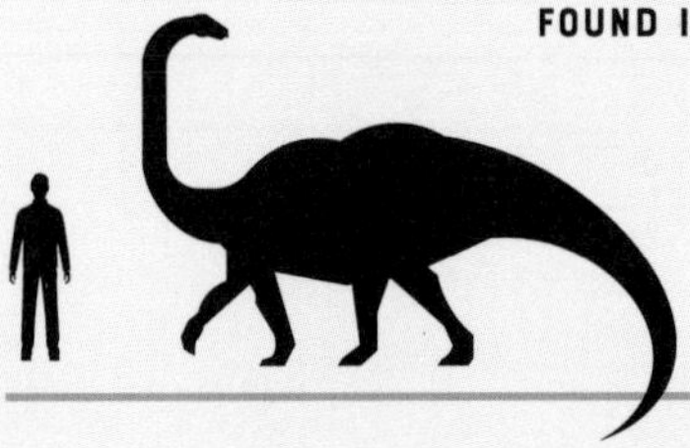

METRIACANTHOSAURUS

(met-ree-a-kan-tho-sore-us)
MODERATELY-SPINED LIZARD

A large meat-eater, *Metriacanthosaurus* lived alongside *Megalosaurus* (page 103) and probably competed with it for food. For a long time, it was actually thought to be the same dinosaur as *Megalosaurus*, but in the 1960s scientists reviewed the bones and realized it was its very own type of dinosaur.

LENGTH: 27 ft

DIET: Carnivorous

WHEN IT LIVED: Late Jurassic (159-154 MYA)

FOUND IN: England

MICROCERATUS

(mike-ro-serr-ah-tops) **TINY-HORNED-FACE ARAL LIZARD**

Microceratops was first named in 1953 but, 50 years later, scientists realized that the name had already taken by a species of beetle, so, in 2008, the name was changed to *Microceratus*. We do not know how large this dinosaur would have grown to be, because the only fossils we know of come from a juvenile dinosaur. However, it is thought that it was rather small and agile, and able to evade predators simply by running away.

LENGTH: About 1.5 ft

DIET: Herbivorous

WHEN IT LIVED: Late Cretaceous (86-66 MYA)

FOUND IN: People's Republic of China and Mongolia

MICROPACHYCEPHALOSAURUS

(mike-row-pak-ee-keff-ah-loh-sore-us) **TINY THICK-HEADED LIZARD**

LENGTH: 2 ft

DIET: Herbivorous

WHEN IT LIVED: Late Cretaceous (84-71 MYA)

FOUND IN: People's Republic of China

FIGURE 102: *Microceratus*

FIGURE 101: *Metriacanthosaurus*

MICRORAPTOR

(MIKE-row-rap-tor) **TINY PLUNDERER**

Microraptor was a feathered dinosaur that not only had feathers on its arms but on its legs, too. It may have been capable of gliding through the air, and probably hunted in the forests, eating insects or small reptiles. It was close to the modern birds of today on the family tree, and has provided scientists with a good deal of information on how flight may have first evolved.

LENGTH: 2.5 ft

DIET: Carnivore

WHEN IT LIVED: Early Cretaceous (125-122 MYA)

FOUND IN: People's Republic of China

FIGURE 103: *Microraptor*

MINMI

(min-mie) **NAMED AFTER MINMI CROSSING, QUEENSLAND**

LENGTH: 10 ft

DIET: Herbivorous

WHEN IT LIVED: Early Cretaceous (121-112 MYA)

FOUND IN: Australia

FIGURE 104: *Monolophosaurus*

MONOLOPHOSAURUS

(mono-Loh-foh-sore-us) **SINGLE-CRESTED LIZARD**

The "mono" part of this dinosaur's name refers to the single, bony crest on its skull, which appears to be different to the double crest than can be seen in closely related dinosaurs like *Dilophosaurus* (page 54). It was a fearsome meat-eater and probably hunted sauropods like *Bellusaurus* (page 32) in the region that is now China.

LENGTH: 19 ft

DIET: Carnivorous

WHEN IT LIVED: Mid Jurassic (180-159 MYA)

FOUND IN: People's Republic of China

MONONYKUS

(mono-Nike-us) **SINGLE CLAW**

LENGTH: 3 ft

DIET: Unknown

WHEN IT LIVED: Late Cretaceous (81-68 MYA)

FOUND IN: People's Republic of China and Mongolia

MUSSAURUS

(moos-SORE-us) **MOUSE LIZARD**

Mussaurus was named the "mouse lizard" because the first one ever found was very, very small. We now know that this sauropod dinosaur actually grew to be very, very large—like other sauropods—and that the first fossil specimen was only of a young *Mussaurus*. It would not have been hatched out of its egg for very long before it was buried and fossilized.

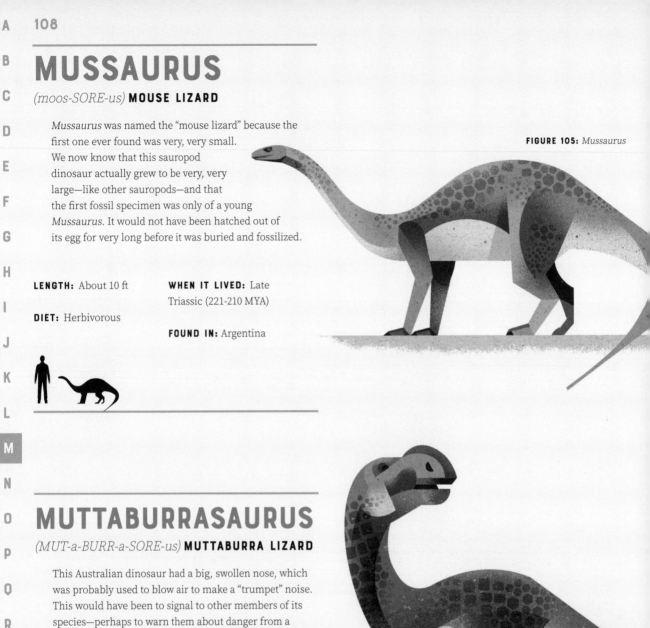

FIGURE 105: *Mussaurus*

LENGTH: About 10 ft

DIET: Herbivorous

WHEN IT LIVED: Late Triassic (221-210 MYA)

FOUND IN: Argentina

MUTTABURRASAURUS

(MUT-a-BURR-a-SORE-us) **MUTTABURRA LIZARD**

This Australian dinosaur had a big, swollen nose, which was probably used to blow air to make a "trumpet" noise. This would have been to signal to other members of its species—perhaps to warn them about danger from a predator, or to find each other when they had walked out of sight. A fossil specimen of *Muttaburasaurus* was once found where all of the bones had been transformed over time into shiny, opal stone.

LENGTH: 23 ft

DIET: Herbivorous

WHEN IT LIVED: Early Cretaceous (110-100 MYA)

FOUND IN: Australia

FIGURE 106: *Muttaburrasaurus*

N

NANOTYRANNUS

(nan-oh-tie-ran-us) **TINY TYRANT**

LENGTH: 16 ft

DIET: Carnivorous

WHEN IT LIVED: Late Cretaceous (67-65 MYA)

FOUND IN: USA

NANSHIUNGOSAURUS

(nahn-shyung-oh-sore-us) **NANXIONG LIZARD**

LENGTH: 14-17 ft

DIET: Omnivorous

WHEN IT LIVED: Late Cretaceous (84-71 MYA)

FOUND IN: People's Republic of China

NEDOCERATOPS

(ned-O-seh-rah-tops) **INSUFFICIENT-HORNED FACE**

A close relative of *Triceratops* (page 165), *Nedoceratops* would have looked similar in nearly every way. The only difference was in the number of horns on their heads. *Triceratops* had three horns—two above the eyes and one on the nose—while *Nedoceratops* had two horns over the eyes, but no nasal horn. Like *Triceratops*, it would have been a slow-moving, four-legged herbivore.

LENGTH: Up to 20 ft

DIET: Herbivorous

WHEN IT LIVED: Late Cretaceous (66 MYA)

FOUND IN: USA

FIGURE 107: *Nedoceratops*

FIGURE 108: *Neovenator*

NEMEGTOSAURUS

(nem-egg-tow-sore-us) **NEMEGT LIZARD**

LENGTH: 43 ft

DIET: Herbivorous

WHEN IT LIVED: Late Cretaceous (72-68 MYA)

FOUND IN: Mongolia

NEOVENATOR

(nee-oh-ve-nay-tor) **NEW HUNTER**

Fossils of *Neovenator* suggest that it was one of the largest theropod dinosaurs in Europe. Even though it would have been large for a theropod, it was probably quite a slender dinosaur, which means that it would have been lightweight enough to move quickly across the Early Cretacous landscape. This suggests it probably hunted fast-moving prey.

LENGTH: 24 ft

DIET: Carnivorous

WHEN IT LIVED: Early Cretaceous (127-121 MYA)

FOUND IN: England

NEUQUENSAURUS

(nayoo-ken-oh-sore-us) **NEUQUÉN (RIVER) LIZARD**

Neuquensaurus was a relatively small sauropod that had hardened, bone-like, raised scales on its back, which would have acted as protective armor. This would have been quite unusual among the sauropods, but some of its closest relatives—like *Antarctosaurus* (page 20) and *Saltosaurus* (page 139)—might also have had these.

LENGTH: 32-50 ft

WHEN IT LIVED: Late Cretaceous (71-65 MYA)

DIET: Herbivorous

FOUND IN: Argentina

NIGERSAURUS

(nee-zhayr-sore-us) **NIGER LIZARD**

LENGTH: 50 ft

DIET: Herbivorous

WHEN IT LIVED: Early Cretaceous (121-99 MYA)

FOUND IN: Niger, Algeria and Tunisia

FIGURE 109: *Neuquensaurus*

Letters down left margin: A B C D E F G H I J K L M N O P Q R S T U V W X Y Z

NIPPONOSAURUS

(nip-on-oh-sore-us) **JAPANESE LIZARD**

Discovered back in 1934, this large herbivore belongs to the hadrosaur group of dinosaurs. Like other hadrosaurs, *Nipponosaurus* had a bony crest on top of its skull, which scientists think may have been used for signaling to other members of its species, or to scare away rivals and predators.

LENGTH: About 13 ft

DIET: Herbivorous

WHEN IT LIVED: Late Cretaceous (89-84 MYA)

FOUND IN: Russia

FIGURE 110: *Nipponosaurus*

NOASAURUS

(noh-ah-sore-us) **NORTHWESTERN ARGENTINA LIZARD**

LENGTH: 3-10 ft

DIET: Carnivorous

WHEN IT LIVED: Late Cretaceous (84-65 MYA)

FOUND IN: Argentina

A B C D E F G H I J K L M N O P Q R S T U V W X Y Z

NODOSAURUS

(no-doh-SORE-us) **NODE LIZARD**

LENGTH: 16 ft

DIET: Herbivorous

WHEN IT LIVED: Early Cretaceous (110-100 MYA)

FOUND IN: USA

NOMINGIA

(noh-ming-ee-uh) **NOMINGIIN**

Nomingia was a small- to medium-sized theropod, in the same family as *Oviraptor* (page 119). By comparing it with dinosaurs like *Oviraptor*, scientists can be fairly confident that it would have had a beak and a crest on its skull, as well as a covering of elaborate feathers on its body.

LENGTH: 5 ft

DIET: Omnivorous

WHEN IT LIVED: Late Cretaceous (72-68 MYA)

FOUND IN: Mongolia

FIGURE 111: *Nomingia*

A B C D E F G H I J K L M **N** O P Q R S T U V W X Y Z

FIGURE 112: *Nothronychus*

NOTHRONYCHUS

(noh-thron-i-kus) **SLOTH-LIKE CLAW**

Nothronychus may have evolved over time from being a meat-eater to become a plant-eater. This bizarre-looking creature had a squat body, long neck, and enormous claws on its fingers to hook around branches, a bit like a sloth does today. The way the hips of this dinosaur were put together suggests that it had a big, round belly, which would have been suited to digesting plants. This is because plants take longer to digest than meat, so a diet of plants requires a larger digestive system.

LENGTH: 17 ft

DIET: Omnivorous

WHEN IT LIVED: Late Cretaceous (94-89 MYA)

FOUND IN: USA

NQWEBASAURUS

(n-qu-web-ah-sore-us) **NQWEBA LIZARD**

LENGTH: 3 ft

DIET: Carnivorous

WHEN IT LIVED: Early Cretaceous (159-132 MYA)

FOUND IN: South Africa

OMEISAURUS
(oh-mee-sore-us) **OMEI LIZARD**

Based on the number of fossils found, *Omeisaurus* seems to have been the most common sauropod in Middle Jurassic China. It would have traveled in herds, browsing in open areas for shrubby ferns, but could also have reached the highest of trees with its long neck. It looked very similar to its close relative *Mamenchisaurus* (page 100), which had an even longer neck.

LENGTH: 65 ft

DIET: Herbivorous

WHEN IT LIVED: Mid Jurassic (169-159 MYA)

FOUND IN: People's Republic of China

OPISTHOCOELICAUDIA
(o-pis-tho-seel-i-cawd-ee-a) **HOLLOW-BACKED TAIL**

LENGTH: 40 ft

DIET: Herbivorous

WHEN IT LIVED: Late Cretaceous (72-68 MYA)

FOUND IN: Mongolia

FIGURE 113: *Omeisaurus*

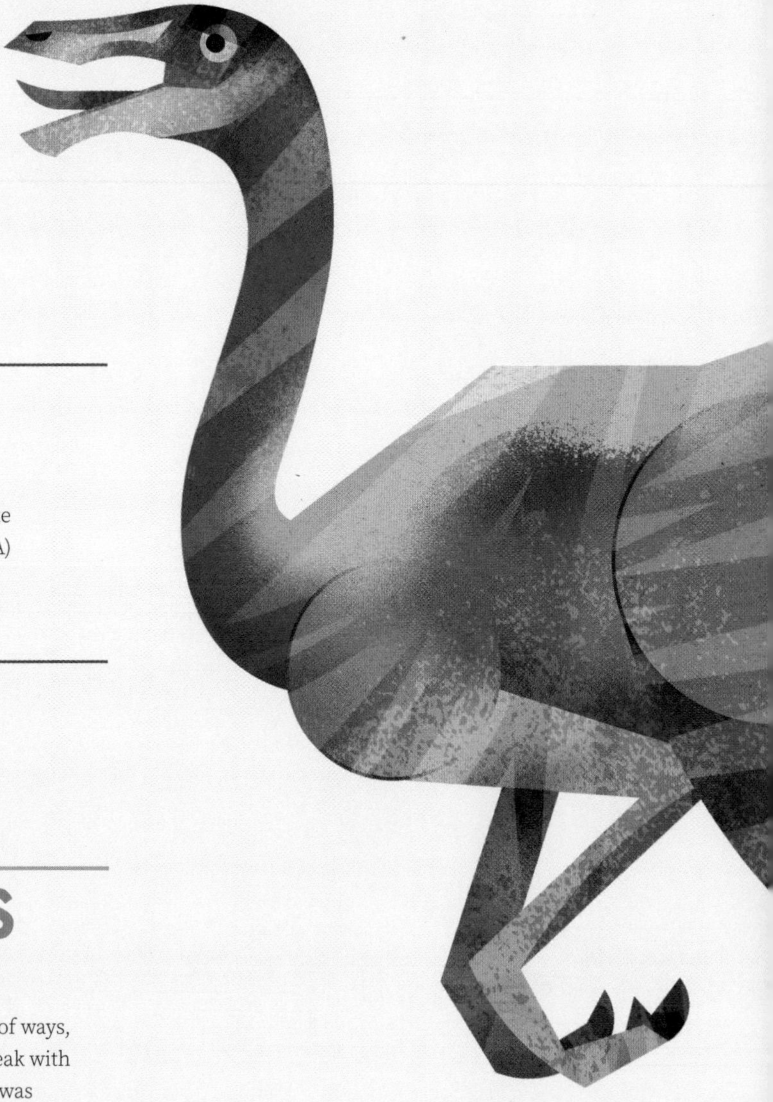

ORNITHOLESTES

(or-nith-oh-LES-teez) **BIRD ROBBER**

LENGTH: 6.5 ft

DIET: Carnivorous

WHEN IT LIVED: Late Jurassic (150-144 MYA)

FOUND IN: USA

ORNITHOMIMUS

(orn-ith-oh-mime-uss) **BIRD MIMIC**

Ornithomimus looked like a bird in a number of ways, particularly in the way it stood. It also had a beak with no teeth at the end of its skull. *Ornithomimus* was probably a very good runner, and would have been agile enough to evade predators like *Daspletosaurus* (page 51)—which lived alongside it in the Cretaceous Period of North America.

LENGTH: 13 ft

DIET: Omnivorous

WHEN IT LIVED: Late Cretaceous (74-65 MYA)

FOUND IN: Canada and USA

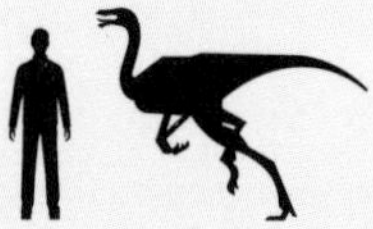

FIGURE 114: *Ornithomimus*

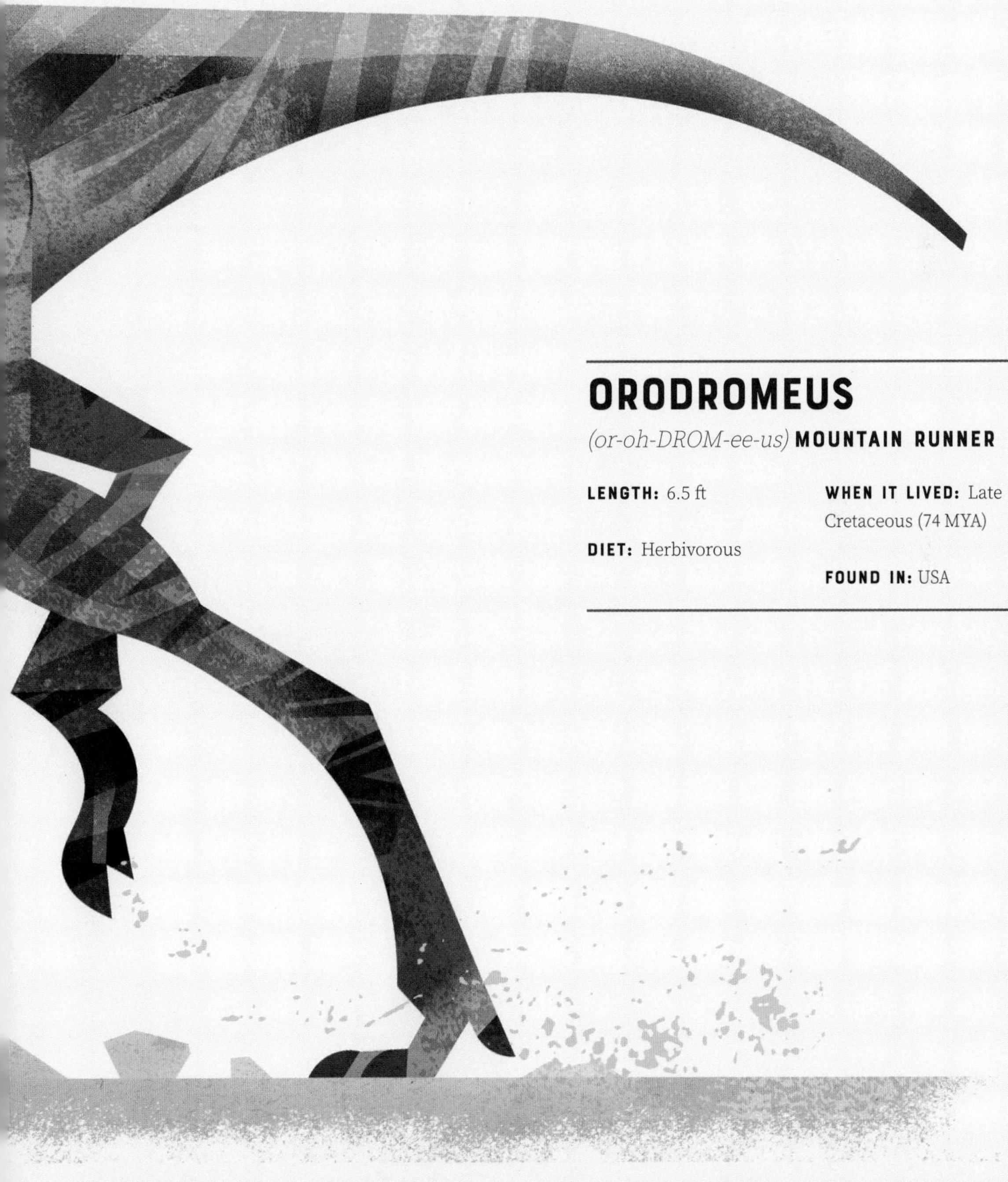

ORODROMEUS

(or-oh-DROM-ee-us) **MOUNTAIN RUNNER**

LENGTH: 6.5 ft

DIET: Herbivorous

WHEN IT LIVED: Late Cretaceous (74 MYA)

FOUND IN: USA

ORYCTODROMEUS

(or-ik-tow-drohm-ee-us) **DIGGING RUNNER**

The fossil remains of this dinosaur were found in its burrow, which shows that some dinosaurs were capable of burrowing underground. Such a burrow might have been used for rearing young, hiding from predators or simply to cope with high or low temperatures on the surface. *Oryctodromeus* was a rather small herbivore, and may have lived in family groups for protection, just like many of today's herbivores.

LENGTH: 7 ft

DIET: Herbivorous

WHEN IT LIVED: Late Cretaceous (99-94 MYA)

FOUND IN: USA

FIGURE 115: *Oryctodromeus*

OTHNIELIA

(oth-ni-ee-lee-a) **FOR OTHNIEL [MARSH]**

LENGTH: 4.5 ft

DIET: Herbivorous

WHEN IT LIVED: Late Jurassic (154-142 MYA)

FOUND IN: USA

A B C D E F G H I J K L M N O P Q R S T U V W X Y Z

OURANOSAURUS

(oo-RAH-noh-sore-us) **BRAVE MONITOR LIZARD**

LENGTH: 23 ft

DIET: Herbivorous

WHEN IT LIVED: Early Cretaceous (115-100 MYA)

FOUND IN: Niger

OVIRAPTOR

(OH-vee-RAP-tor) **EGG THIEF**

The curved upper and lower jaws of *Oviraptor* would have been able to crush some of the hardest of objects. This suggests that this dinosaur may have eaten eggs, or fed on fish and shellfish by cracking them open. Scientists originally thought that this dinosaur stole eggs because it was found near fossilized eggs—hence its name. However, some more recent finds have suggested that this animal was actually guarding the eggs, just as modern birds do.

LENGTH: 6.5 ft

DIET: Omnivorous

WHEN IT LIVED: Late Cretaceous (85-75 MYA)

FOUND IN: Mongolia

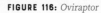

FIGURE 116: *Oviraptor*

P

PACHYCEPHALOSAURUS

(pack-ee-kef-ah-lo-sore-us) **THICK-HEADED LIZARD**

Pachycephalosaurus is an unusual-looking dinosaur. It stood on two legs, had a beak for cropping plants, and on its head was a large dome surrounded by spikes and bumps. Some scientists think that this dome was used in head-butting contests, similar to the way modern-day rams use their horns, while others think that it may have been used for display. It could be that it was used for many things—like the antlers of modern-day deer, which are used both for fighting with other deer and for display.

LENGTH: 26 ft

DIET: Herbivorous

WHEN IT LIVED: Late Cretaceous (76-65 MYA)

FOUND IN: Canada and USA

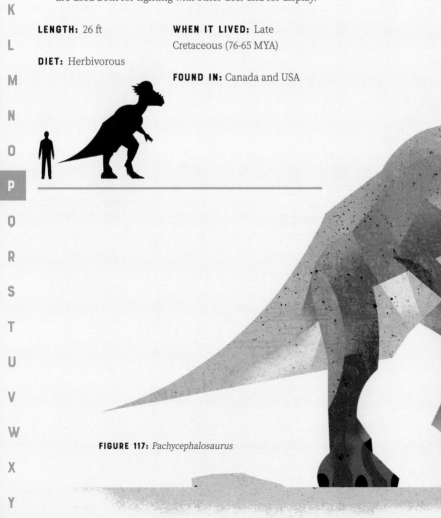

FIGURE 117: *Pachycephalosaurus*

FIGURE 118: *Pachyrhinosaurus*

PACHYRHINOSAURUS

(pack-ee-RINE-oh-sore-us) **THICK-NOSED LIZARD**

Pachyrhinosaurus was a ceratopsian dinosaur, like *Triceratops* (page 165). However, it did not have a large horn on its nose, but instead had a bulky and rough area of flat bone. *Pachyrhinosaurus* lived in the cold, very far north of North America, so it is often illustrated with a coat of warm feather-like structures, but no evidence actually exists to prove it had this kind of feather coating.

LENGTH: 20 ft

WHEN IT LIVED: Late Cretaceous (76-74 MYA)

DIET: Herbivorous

FOUND IN: Canada

PANOPLOSAURUS

(pan-op-loh-sore-us) **FULLY-ARMORED LIZARD**

LENGTH: 23 ft

WHEN IT LIVED: Late Cretaceous (79-75 MYA)

DIET: Herbivorous

FOUND IN: Canada and USA

PANTYDRACO

(pant-ee-drak-oh) **PANT-Y-FFYNNON DRAGON**

LENGTH: 10 ft

WHEN IT LIVED: Early Jurassic (208-201 MYA)

DIET: Herbivorous

FOUND IN: Wales

PARALITITAN

(pa-ral-i-tie-tuhn) **TIDAL GIANT**

LENGTH: 92 ft

DIET: Herbivorous

WHEN IT LIVED: Late Cretaceous (99-94 MYA)

FOUND IN: Egypt

PARASAUROLOPHUS

(pa-ra-saw-ROL-off-us) **LIKE SAUROLOPHUS**

Parasaurolophus had a broad, flat mouth for eating plants and a very unique skull: Extending backward from the back of its head was a long crest, which was hollow on the inside, like a pipe. Air could be blown through chambers inside this crest and it is thought that this action would have made a loud noise that could be heard for many miles around. It is possible that this is how these dinosaurs communicated with one another.

LENGTH: 36 ft

DIET: Herbivorous

WHEN IT LIVED: Late Cretaceous (76-74 MYA)

FOUND IN: Canada and USA

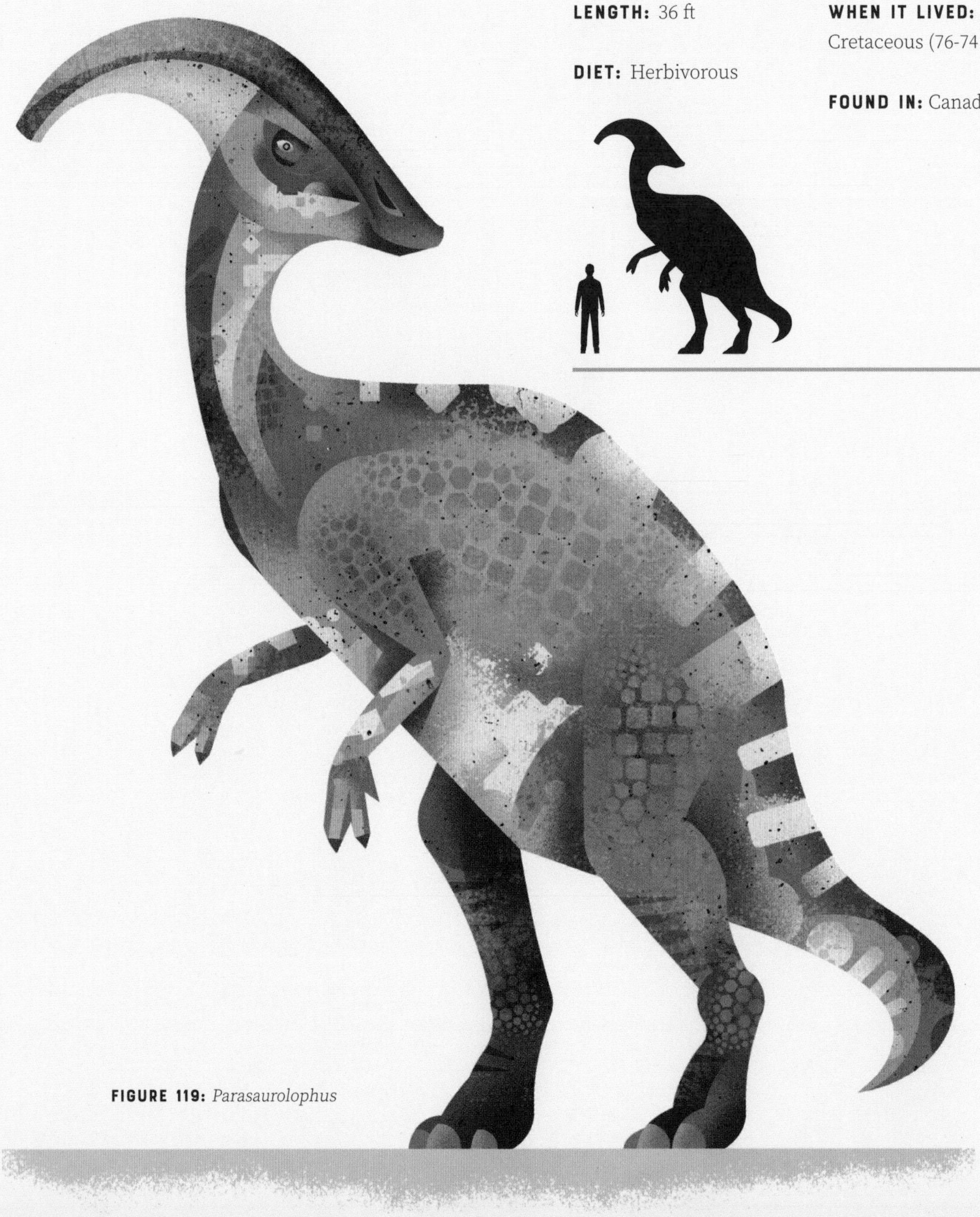

FIGURE 119: *Parasaurolophus*

PARKSOSAURUS

(PARKS-oh-SORE-us) **PARK'S LIZARD**

LENGTH: 10 ft

DIET: Herbivorous

WHEN IT LIVED: Late Cretaceous (76-74 MYA)

FOUND IN: Canada

PATAGOSAURUS

(pat-ag-oh-sore-us) **PATAGONIAN LIZARD**

Many *Patagosaurus* skeletons have been found. From these, we know that this dinosaur was a large, four-legged herbivore, and that it must have been capable of stripping leaves from whole areas of forest with its many peg-like teeth. It would have been a very slow-moving dinosaur, and relied on its size to protect itself from predators such as *Piatnitzkysaurus* (page 125).

LENGTH: 60 ft

DIET: Herbivorous

WHEN IT LIVED: Mid Jurassic (164-159 MYA)

FOUND IN: Argentina

FIGURE 120: *Patagosaurus*

A B C D E F G H I J K L M N O P Q R S T U V W X Y Z

PEGOMASTAX

(peg-o-mas-tahks) **STRONG JAW**

LENGTH: 1.5-2 ft

WHEN IT LIVED: Early Jurassic (200-190 MYA)

DIET: Herbivorous

FOUND IN: South Africa

PELICANIMIMUS

(pel-e-kan-i-mim-us) **PELICAN MIMIC**

Pelecanimimus had more than 200 very small, fine teeth in its mouth, which would have given it a bite that cut and ripped. The fossil that was first used to describe the species—which is known as a "holotype"—was well preserved, showing scientists very clearly that this dinosaur had a throat pouch similar to those seen in today's pelicans.

LENGTH: 6.5-8 ft

WHEN IT LIVED: Early Cretaceous (127-121 MYA)

DIET: Carnivorous

FOUND IN: Spain

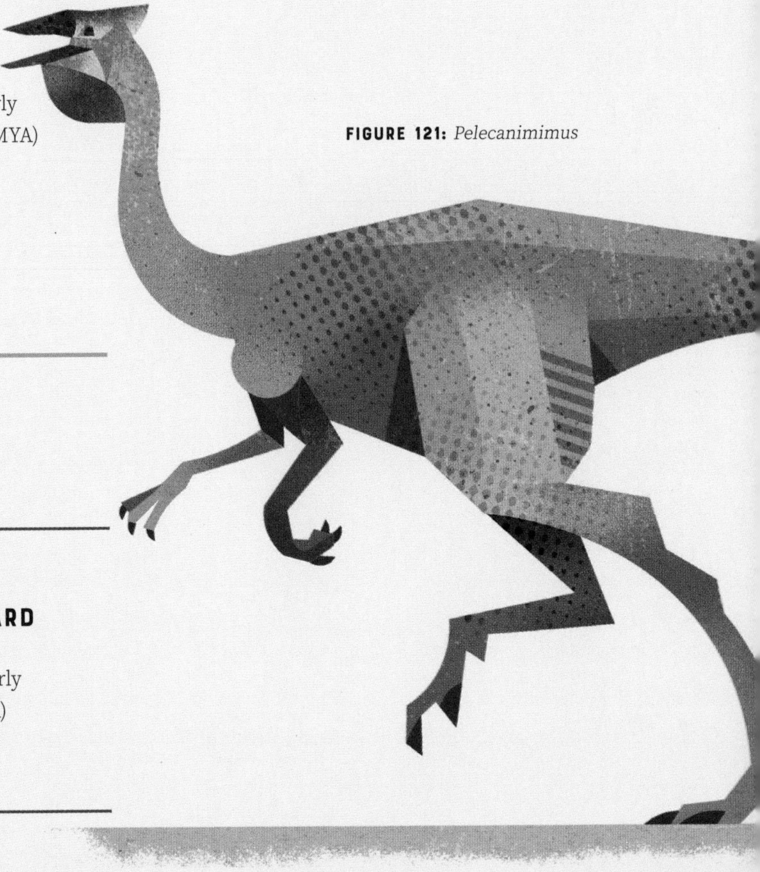

FIGURE 121: *Pelecanimimus*

PELOROSAURUS

(pel-oh-ROW-sore-us) **MONSTROUS LIZARD**

LENGTH: About 82 ft

WHEN IT LIVED: Early Cretaceous (125 MYA)

DIET: Herbivorous

FOUND IN: England

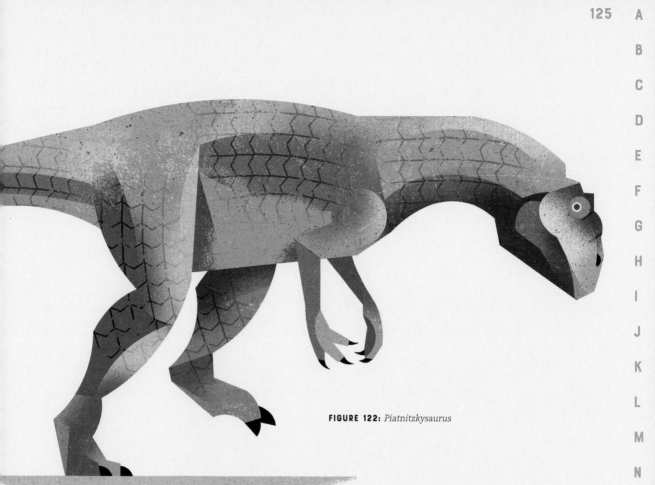

FIGURE 122: *Piatnitzkysaurus*

PENTACERATOPS

(pent-ah-ker-ah-tops) **FIVE-HORNED FACE**

LENGTH: 22 ft

DIET: Herbivorous

WHEN IT LIVED: Late Cretaceous (76-74 MYA)

FOUND IN: USA

PIATNITZKYSAURUS

(pye-at-nits-key-sore-us) **PIATNITZKY'S LIZARD**

Piatnitzkysaurus is closely related to the theropod family that contains the predators *Allosaurus* (page 14) and *Megalosaurus* (page 103). *Piatnitzkysaurus* would have stood on two legs, which would have each been about the length of a fully grown human. It had longer arms than the theropod *Tyrannosaurus* (page 169), and also had more fingers on each hand.

LENGTH: 14 ft

DIET: Carnivorous

WHEN IT LIVED: Late Jurassic (164-159 MYA)

FOUND IN: Argentina

PINACOSAURUS

(pin-ak-oh-sore-us) **PLANK LIZARD**

LENGTH: 16 ft

WHEN IT LIVED: Late Cretaceous (81-75 MYA)

DIET: Herbivorous

FOUND IN: People's Republic of China and Mongolia

PISANOSAURUS

(pie-sahn-oh-sore-us) **PISANO'S LIZARD**

Pisanosaurus is not known from much fossil material, and what does exist is so badly damaged that it is very hard for scientists to interpret. Some think it is an ornithischian (dinosaurs with hip bones like a bird's), while others think that it might not be a dinosaur at all—just a close cousin of dinosaurs. All scientists can say for certain about this creature is that it was a small animal that ate plants.

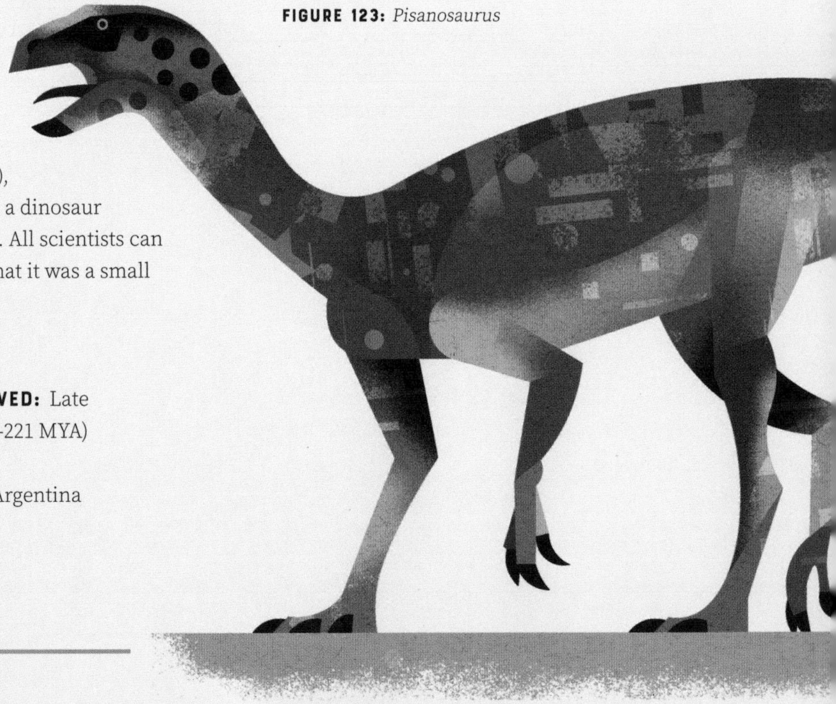

FIGURE 123: *Pisanosaurus*

LENGTH: 3 ft

WHEN IT LIVED: Late Triassic (227-221 MYA)

DIET: Herbivorous

FOUND IN: Argentina

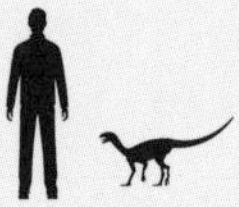

FIGURE 124: *Platyceratops*

PLATYCERATOPS

(plat-ee-serra-tops) **FLAT-HORNED FACE**

Platyceratops is only known from fossils of a skull and lower jawbone. Scientists currently cannot agree about whether this dinosaur is its own species or not, because it may in fact be the same animal as *Bagaceratops* (page 29). No matter the answer, we know it was a small herbivore that belonged to the ceratopsian family of dinosaurs—which had parrot-like beaks, bony frills, and horned faces.

LENGTH: 6.5-10 ft

DIET: Herbivorous

WHEN IT LIVED: Late Cretaceous (75-72 MYA)

FOUND IN: Mongolia

PLATEOSAURUS

(plat-ee-oh-sore-us) **FLAT LIZARD**

LENGTH: 23 ft

DIET: Herbivorous

WHEN IT LIVED: Late Triassic (210 MYA)

FOUND IN: Germany, France, and Switzerland

A B C D E F G H I J K L M N O P Q R S T U V W X Y Z

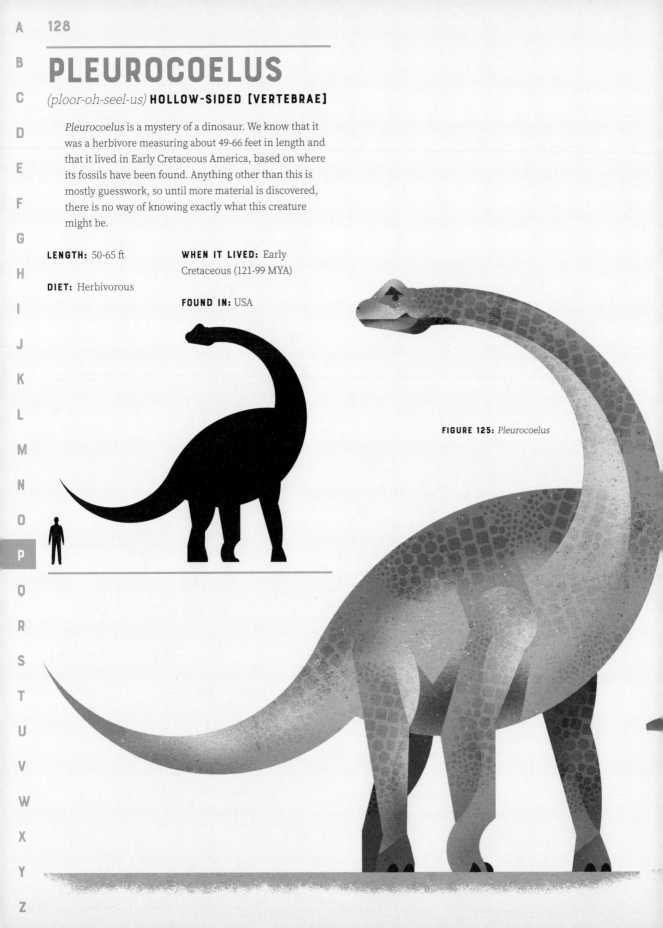

PLEUROCOELUS

(ploor-oh-seel-us) **HOLLOW-SIDED [VERTEBRAE]**

Pleurocoelus is a mystery of a dinosaur. We know that it was a herbivore measuring about 49-66 feet in length and that it lived in Early Cretaceous America, based on where its fossils have been found. Anything other than this is mostly guesswork, so until more material is discovered, there is no way of knowing exactly what this creature might be.

LENGTH: 50-65 ft

DIET: Herbivorous

WHEN IT LIVED: Early Cretaceous (121-99 MYA)

FOUND IN: USA

FIGURE 125: *Pleurocoelus*

PODOKESAURUS

(po-doh-kee-sore-us) **SWIFT-FOOTED LIZARD**

LENGTH: 3 ft

DIET: Carnivorous

WHEN IT LIVED: Mid Jurassic (195-180 MYA)

FOUND IN: USA

POEKILOPLEURON

(peek-i-loh-ploor-on) **VARIED RIBS**

LENGTH: 30 ft

DIET: Carnivorous

WHEN IT LIVED: Mid Jurassic (169-164 MYA)

FOUND IN: France

POLACANTHUS

(pol-a-KAN-thus) **MANY SPINES**

Polacanthus was an ankylosaur, so it would have been covered in armor to protect it from predators. It had spikes along most of its body and a shield-like structure covering its hips, to prevent attacks from predators that could bite down from above. Just like its close relative *Nodosaurus* (page 113), it would have lacked the large club on its tail that would be seen in later ankylosaurs, such as *Ankylosaurus* (page 18).

LENGTH: 16 ft

DIET: Herbivorous

WHEN IT LIVED: Early Cretaceous (125 MYA)

FOUND IN: England

FIGURE 126: *Polacanthus*

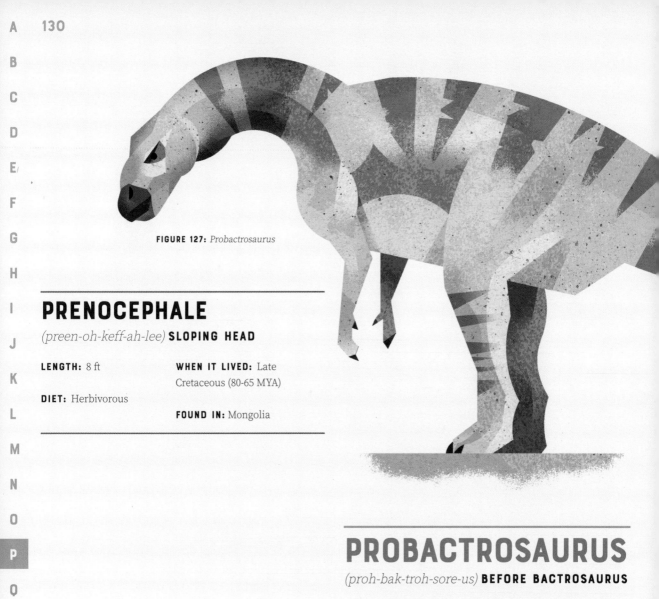

FIGURE 127: *Probactrosaurus*

PRENOCEPHALE

(preen-oh-keff-ah-lee) **SLOPING HEAD**

LENGTH: 8 ft

DIET: Herbivorous

WHEN IT LIVED: Late Cretaceous (80-65 MYA)

FOUND IN: Mongolia

PROBACTROSAURUS

(proh-bak-troh-sore-us) **BEFORE BACTROSAURUS**

Sometimes nicknamed "the Asian Iguanodon," this medium-sized plant-eater would have wandered the Late Cretaceous plains of what is now China, searching for low-growing vegetation to pick at with its beak. Like *Iguanodon* (page 83), it had very complex teeth, fused into a big flat block for grinding up the plant matter that it ate. But unlike most dinosaurs, *Probactrosaurus* could chew side to side, as well as up and down.

LENGTH: 20 ft

DIET: Herbivorous

WHEN IT LIVED: Late Cretaceous (121-99 MYA)

FOUND IN: People's Republic of China

PROCERATOSAURUS

(proh-ker-at-oh-sore-us) **BEFORE CERATOSAURUS**

LENGTH: 13 ft

DIET: Carnivorous

WHEN IT LIVED: Mid Jurassic (169-164 MYA)

FOUND IN: England

PROCOMPSOGNATHUS

(pro-comp-sog-nay-thus) **BEFORE COMPSOGNATHUS**

The only fossil of *Procompsognathus* is poorly preserved but we know it had large, clawed hands and a long snout. It was a very small theropod, and probably relied on speed to catch its prey, which ranged from dragonflies to little lizards. *Procompsognathus* was named because it looked very similar to *Compsognathus* (page 47), but appeared millions of years before it.

LENGTH: 3 ft

DIET: Carnivorous

WHEN IT LIVED: Late Triassic (221-210 MYA)

FOUND IN: Germany

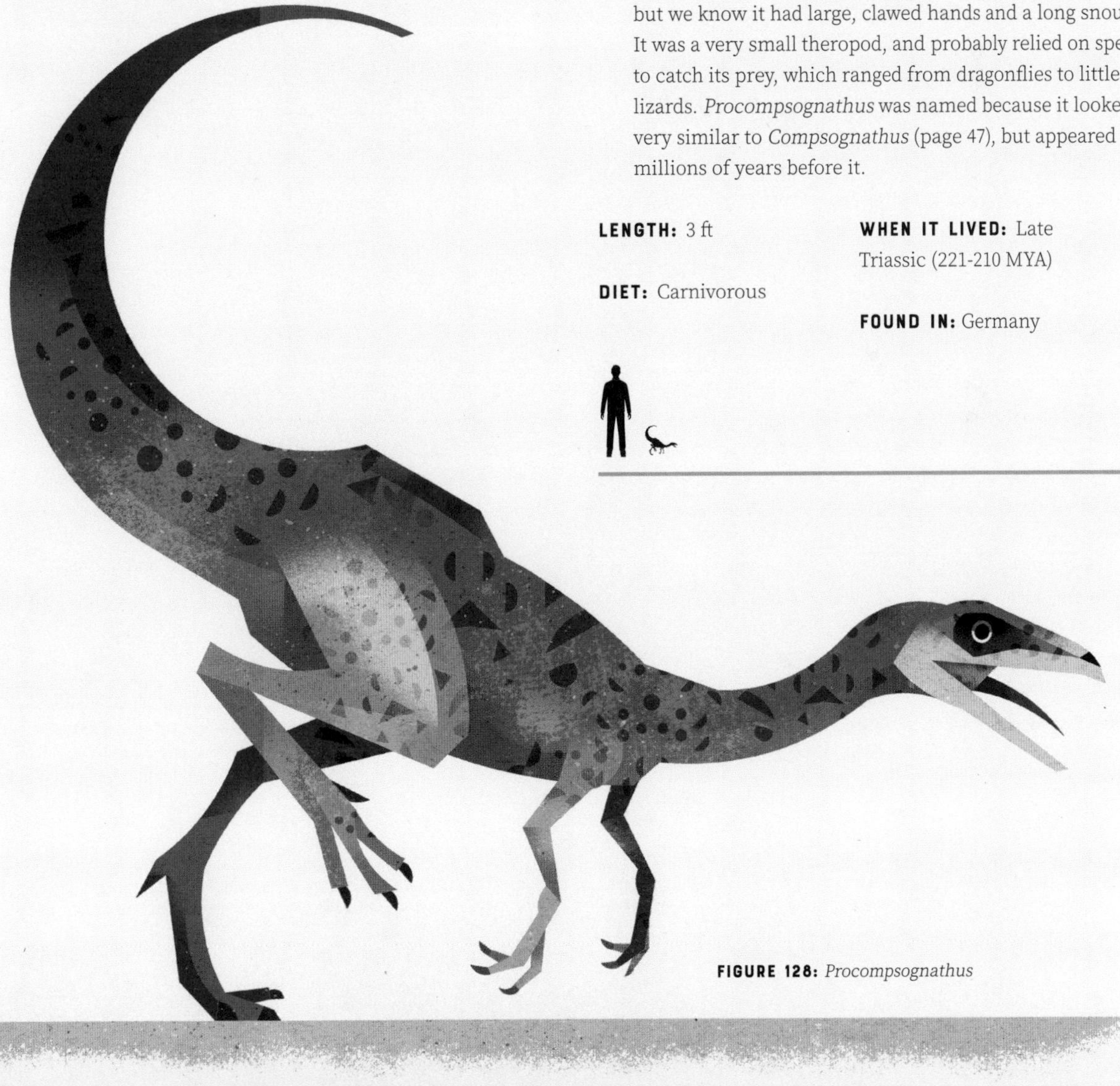

FIGURE 128: *Procompsognathus*

FIGURE 129: *Prosaurolophus*

PROSAUROLOPHUS

(proh-sore-oh-lof-us) **BEFORE LIZARD CREST [SAUROLOPHUS]**

Prosaurolophus is known from the skeletons of around 24 individuals. Some of these skeletons were "articulated," which means that they were found undisturbed and joined together in the positions they would have been in life. It is possible to tell from the fossils that this dinosaur would have lived in groups for at least part of the year. As a medium to large hadrosaur, it only ate plants and had a triangular crest in front of its eyes.

LENGTH: 25 ft

DIET: Herbivorous

WHEN IT LIVED: Late Cretaceous (77-75 MYA)

FOUND IN: Canada and USA

PROTARCHAEOPTERYX

(pro-tark-ee-op-ter-iks) **BEFORE ARCHAEOPTERYX**

LENGTH: 6.5 ft

DIET: Carnivorous

WHEN IT LIVED: Early Cretaceous (122-120 MYA)

FOUND IN: People's Republic of China

PROTOCERATOPS

(pro-toe-ser-ah-tops) **FIRST HORNED FACE**

Protoceratops was a small ceratopsian. It was much smaller than later ceratopsians like *Triceratops* (page 165), and although it had a bony neck frill it did not have horns. Incredibly, one fossil of a *Protoceratops* actually shows it being attacked by a *Velociraptor* (page 172). They were probably buried by a sandstorm in the middle of their struggle and so were preserved that way.

LENGTH: 6 ft

DIET: Herbivorous

WHEN IT LIVED: Late Cretaceous (85-80 MYA)

FOUND IN: People's Republic of China and Mongolia

FIGURE 130: *Protoceratops*

A B C D E F G H I J K L M N O P Q R S T U V W X Y Z

PROTOHADROS

(proh-toh-had-ros) **FIRST HADROSAUR**

This was a very early duck-billed hadrosaur. Its name roughly means "first hadrosaur" because of the ideas that scientists have about where it fits into the dinosaur family tree. Like other, later hadrosaurs, this dinosaur was a slow-moving herbivore, and probably lived in herds.

LENGTH: 20 ft

DIET: Herbivorous

WHEN IT LIVED: Late Cretaceous (99-94 MYA)

FOUND IN: USA

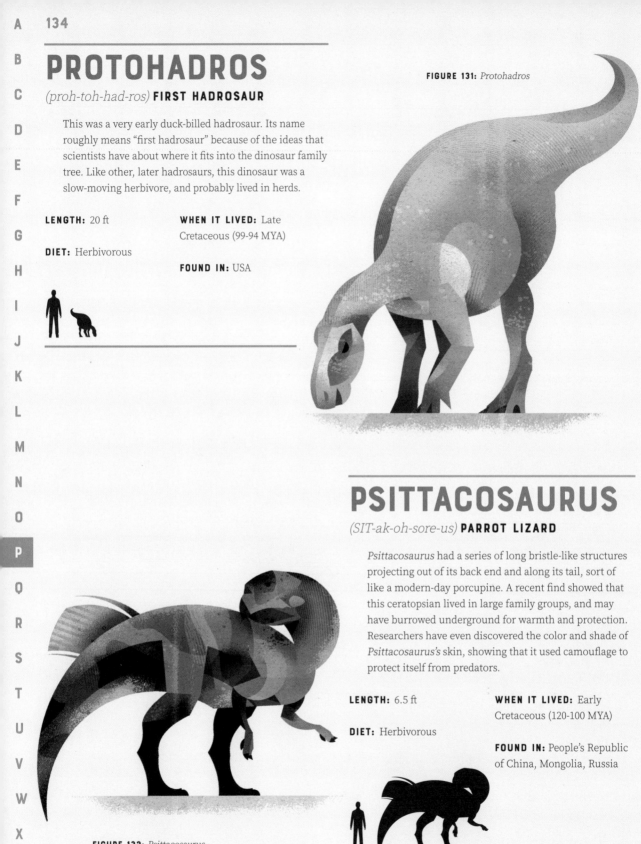

FIGURE 131: *Protohadros*

PSITTACOSAURUS

(SIT-ak-oh-sore-us) **PARROT LIZARD**

Psittacosaurus had a series of long bristle-like structures projecting out of its back end and along its tail, sort of like a modern-day porcupine. A recent find showed that this ceratopsian lived in large family groups, and may have burrowed underground for warmth and protection. Researchers have even discovered the color and shade of *Psittacosaurus's* skin, showing that it used camouflage to protect itself from predators.

LENGTH: 6.5 ft

DIET: Herbivorous

WHEN IT LIVED: Early Cretaceous (120-100 MYA)

FOUND IN: People's Republic of China, Mongolia, Russia

FIGURE 132: *Psittacosaurus*

QUAESITOSAURUS

(kwee-siet-oh-sore-us) **EXTRAORDINARY LIZARD**

LENGTH: 75 ft

WHEN IT LIVED: Late Cretaceous (86-84 MYA)

DIET: Herbivorous

FOUND IN: Mongolia

REBBACHISAURUS

(re-bash-i-sore-us) **REBBACH LIZARD**

Rebbachisaurus was a very heavy and slow-moving animal. It had huge claws on its rear feet and a whiplike tail. Although it looked a lot like *Diplodocus* (page 55), it had large spines all the way along its backbone. These spines might have supported a "sail," which would have made it look much bigger than it actually was—helping it to scare away predators.

LENGTH: 65 ft

WHEN IT LIVED: Late Cretaceous (112-99 MYA)

DIET: Herbivorous

FOUND IN: Morocco

FIGURE 133: *Rebbachisaurus*

FIGURE 134: *Rhoetosaurus*

RHOETOSAURUS

(reet-oh-sore-us) **RHOETAN LIZARD**

Named after a Titan from Greek mythology, *Rhoetosaurus* was a fittingly large dinosaur. It weighed about 10 tons and was probably about 49 feet long from head to tail. It is one of only a very small number of sauropods known from Australia. It is also one of the most complete dinosaur skeletons to have been found there.

LENGTH: Over 50 ft

DIET: Herbivorous

WHEN IT LIVED: Mid Jurassic (177-169 MYA)

FOUND IN: Australia

RHABDODON

(RAB-doh-don) **ROD TOOTH**

LENGTH: 13 ft

DIET: Herbivorous

WHEN IT LIVED: Late Cretaceous (76-70 MYA)

FOUND IN: Spain, Austria, France, and Romania

FIGURE 135: *Rinchenia*

FIGURE 136: *Rugops*

RINCHENIA

(rin-chen-ee-ah) **RINCHEN**

This dinosaur was originally thought to be a species of *Oviraptor* (page 119). However, even though the two dinosaurs were similar in size, it was later decided that their skeletons were too different for them to come from the same dinosaur. *Rinchenia* had more of a lightweight skeleton than *Oviraptor* and it also had a much taller, dome-like crest on its head.

LENGTH: 8 ft

DIET: Omnivorous

WHEN IT LIVED: Late Cretaceous (72-68 MYA)

FOUND IN: Mongolia and People's Republic of China

RUGOPS

(roo-gops) **WRINKLE FACE**

An almost-complete fossil of *Rugops's* skull has been found. It is quite delicate, with weak teeth, which tells us that *Rugops* was probably a scavenging theropod—it was not built for attacking or preying on other dinosaurs in the same way that theropods like *Tyrannosaurus* (page 169) were. Its skull shows that lots of blood vessels would have run along its face, which gives the skull a "wrinkled" effect.

LENGTH: 23 ft

DIET: Carnivorous

WHEN IT LIVED: Late Cretaceous (95 MYA)

FOUND IN: Niger

RIOJASAURUS

(ree-ock-ah-sore-us) **[LA] RIOJA LIZARD**

LENGTH: 17 ft

DIET: Omnivorous

WHEN IT LIVED: Late Triassic (221-210 MYA)

FOUND IN: Argentina

FIGURE 137: *Saltasaurus*

SALTASAURUS

(salt-a-sore-us) **SALTA LIZARD**

Saltasaurus was a titanosaur, which is a particularly huge type of sauropod. Fossils have been found showing that *Saltasaurus* had small, bony nodules in its skin, which prove that titanosaurs had armored plates. *Saltasaurus* was one of the last sauropods to walk the planet, living just before this group of dinosaurs became extinct.

LENGTH: 40 ft

DIET: Herbivorous

WHEN IT LIVED: Late Cretaceous (70-65 MYA)

FOUND IN: Argentina

SAICHANIA

(sigh-CHAN-ee-a) **BEAUTIFUL**

LENGTH: 22 ft

DIET: Herbivorous

WHEN IT LIVED: Late Cretaceous (80 MYA)

FOUND IN: Mongolia

SALTOPUS

(sal-to-pus) **HOPPING FOOT**

Saltopus was a small dinosaur—possibly one of the smallest meat-eating dinosaurs of all time. It was probably under 3 feet in length when it was fully grown, but because of how fragmented its fossils are, scientists cannot be absolutely sure. Some scientists even think *Saltopus* was not even a dinosaur in the first place and that it was just a very close relative of the dinosaurs.

LENGTH: About 3 ft

DIET: Carnivorous

WHEN IT LIVED: Late Triassic (221-210 MYA)

FOUND IN: Scotland

SARCOSAURUS

(sahr-koh-sore-us) **FLESH LIZARD**

LENGTH: 10 ft

DIET: Carnivorous

WHEN IT LIVED: Early Jurassic (202-195 MYA)

FOUND IN: England

FIGURE 138: *Saltopus*

FIGURE 139: *Sauropelta*

SAUROLOPHUS

(SORE-oh-LOAF-us) **RIDGED LIZARD**

LENGTH: 30 ft

WHEN IT LIVED: Late Cretaceous (74-70 MYA)

DIET: Herbivorous

FOUND IN: Canada and Mongolia

SAUROPELTA

(sore-oh-pelt-ah) **LIZARD SHIELD**

The fossils of *Sauropelta* are spectacular, because much of the armor covering that would have protected this ankylosaur in life has been preserved. It had enormous shoulder spines that pointed upward, backward, and out to the sides, protecting its neck from attack from predators like *Deinoychus* (page 52). *Sauropelta* would have been a very slow mover, and probably would not have been very intelligent.

LENGTH: 21 ft

WHEN IT LIVED: Early Cretaceous (121-94 MYA)

DIET: Herbivorous

FOUND IN: USA

A
B
C
D
E
F
G
H
I
J
K
L
M
N
O
P
Q
R
S
T
U
V
W
X
Y
Z

FIGURE 140: *Saurophaganax*

SAUROPHAGANAX

(sore-oh-fag-ah-naks) **KING OF THE LIZARD EATERS**

Saurophaganax's name is very fitting because it was a master of hunting other dinosaurs. It was big, strong, and probably very fast. It lived at the same time—and in the same place—as some of the largest tree-browsing dinosaurs, like *Apatosaurus* (page 20), which probably provided *Saurophaganax* with most of its meals.

LENGTH: 40 ft

DIET: Carnivorous

WHEN IT LIVED: Late Jurassic (154-142 MYA)

FOUND IN: USA

SAURORNITHOIDES

(sore-OR-nith-OID-eez) **BIRD-LIKE LIZARD**

LENGTH: 10 ft

DIET: Carnivorous

WHEN IT LIVED: Late Cretaceous (85-80 MYA)

FOUND IN: Mongolia

SAURORNITHOLESTES

(saw-orn-ith-O-les-tees) **LIZARD BIRD THIEF**

LENGTH: 6.5-10 ft

DIET: Carnivorous

WHEN IT LIVED: Late Cretaceous (77-70 MYA)

FOUND IN: USA and Canada

SCUTELLOSAURUS

(skoo-tell-oh-sore-us) **SMALL SHIELD LIZARD**

One of the earliest of the armored dinosaurs, *Scutellosaurus* was covered in rows and rows of small, bony spikes and bumps that scientists call "scutes." This is why its name begins with "scute." Unusual for an armored dinosaur, *Scutellosaurus* may have walked on just two legs instead of four. But it was also much, much smaller than most of the other dinosaurs of its kind—probably only the size of a domestic dog.

LENGTH: 4 ft

DIET: Herbivorous

WHEN IT LIVED: Early Jurassic (205-202 MYA)

FOUND IN: USA

SCELIDOSAURUS

(skel-EYE-doh-sore-us) **LIMB LIZARD**

LENGTH: 13 ft

DIET: Herbivorous

WHEN IT LIVED: Early Jurassic (208-194 MYA)

FOUND IN: England

FIGURE 141: *Scutellosaurus*

SECERNOSAURUS

(see-ser-noh-sore-us) **SEPARATED LIZARD**

LENGTH: 10 ft

DIET: Herbivorous

WHEN IT LIVED: Late Cretaceous (71-65 MYA)

FOUND IN: Argentina

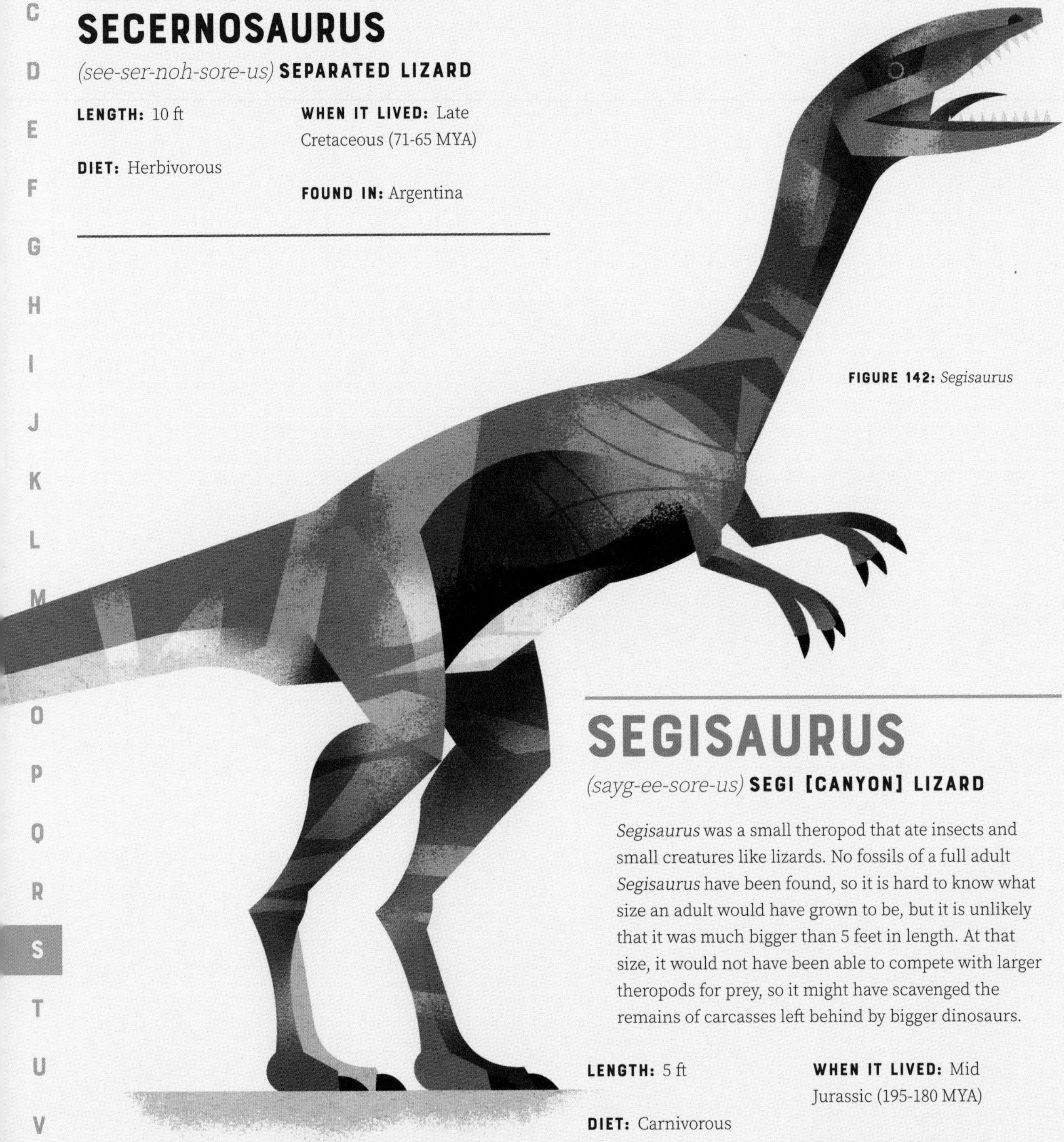

FIGURE 142: *Segisaurus*

SEGISAURUS

(sayg-ee-sore-us) **SEGI [CANYON] LIZARD**

Segisaurus was a small theropod that ate insects and small creatures like lizards. No fossils of a full adult *Segisaurus* have been found, so it is hard to know what size an adult would have grown to be, but it is unlikely that it was much bigger than 5 feet in length. At that size, it would not have been able to compete with larger theropods for prey, so it might have scavenged the remains of carcasses left behind by bigger dinosaurs.

LENGTH: 5 ft

DIET: Carnivorous

WHEN IT LIVED: Mid Jurassic (195-180 MYA)

FOUND IN: USA

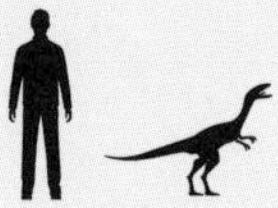

SEGNOSAURUS

(SEG-no-SORE-us) **SLOW LIZARD**

LENGTH: 13 ft

WHEN IT LIVED: Late Cretaceous (97-88 MYA)

DIET: Carnivorous

FOUND IN: Mongolia

SEISMOSAURUS

(SIZE-moh-SORE-us) **EARTH-SHAKING LIZARD**

LENGTH: Over 130 ft

WHEN IT LIVED: Late Jurassic (155-144 MYA)

DIET: Herbivorous

FOUND IN: USA

SHAMOSAURUS

(shah-maw-sore-us) **DESERT LIZARD**

Shamosaurus is named after the Gobi desert in Mongolia, which is where it was found (*sha mo* in Chinese means "sand desert"). We know that it had spines lining its back, a narrow beak, and plates on its head. It was also one of the first armored dinosaurs to have a clubbed tail that it could use to defend itself from predators.

LENGTH: 16 ft

WHEN IT LIVED: Early Cretaceous (121-99 MYA)

DIET: Herbivorous

FOUND IN: Mongolia

FIGURE 143: *Shamosaurus*

SHANAG

(sha-nag) **NAMED AFTER THE DANCERS IN THE BUDDHIST TSAM FESTIVAL**

Even though there are only a few fossil skull fragments of Shanag, scientists can still tell that it was a small theropod and that it was closely related to dinosaurs like *Velociraptor* (page 172). Just like *Velociraptor*, it was a meat-eater that probably had feathers on its body.

LENGTH: 1.5 ft

WHEN IT LIVED: Early Cretaceous (142-126 MYA)

DIET: Carnivorous

FOUND IN: Mongolia

SHANTUNGOSAURUS

(shan-TUN-go-sore-us)
SHANTUNG (SHANDONG) LIZARD

LENGTH: 50 ft

DIET: Herbivorous

WHEN IT LIVED: Late Cretaceous (78-74 MYA)

FOUND IN: People's Republic of China

FIGURE 144: *Shanag*

SHUNOSAURUS

(SHOON-oh-SORE-us) **SHUNO LIZARD**

LENGTH: 32 ft

DIET: Herbivorous

WHEN IT LIVED: Mid Jurassic (170-160 MYA)

FOUND IN: People's Republic of China

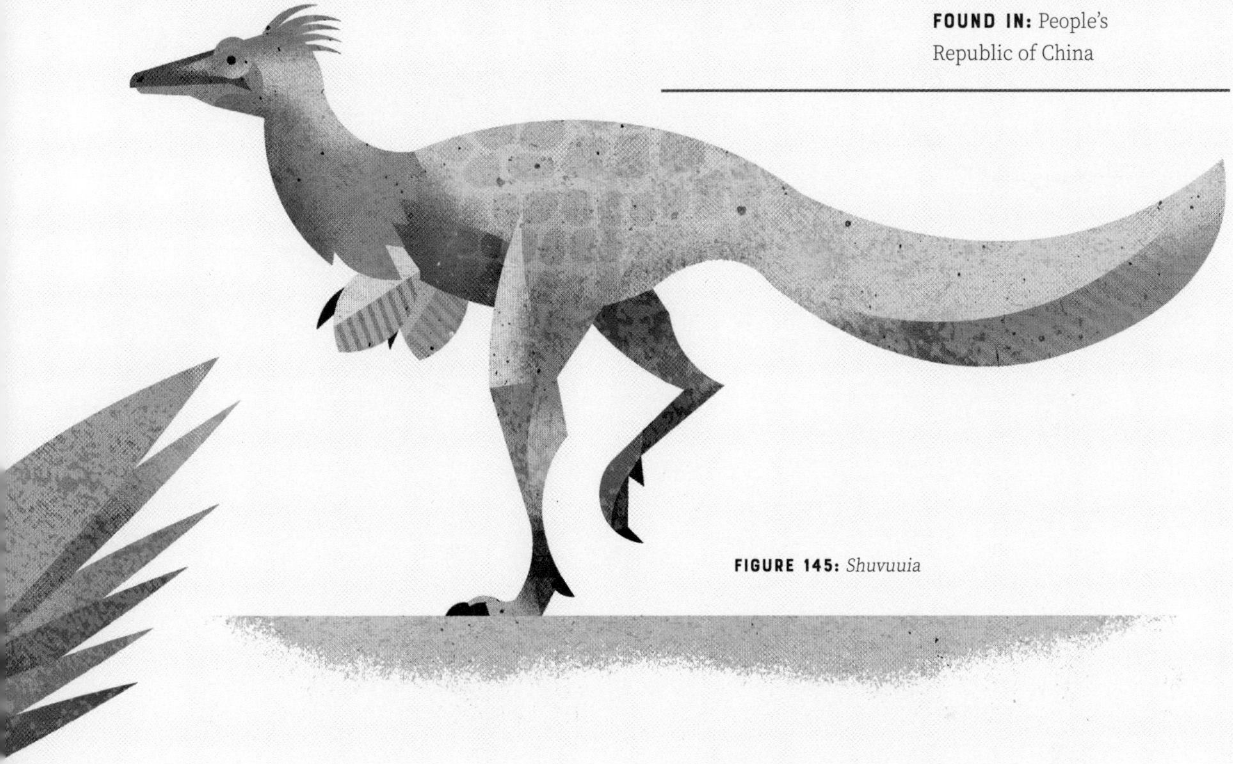

FIGURE 145: *Shuvuuia*

SHUVUUIA

(shu-voo-ee-ah) **BIRD**

This very small desert dinosaur may have had a diet of termites. Interestingly, its lower jaw did not interlock with its skull—which means it was able to open its mouth very wide to eat large prey. This might also have made its jaws flexible enough to reach termites or other insects hiding in tight corners.

LENGTH: 2 ft

DIET: Omnivorous

WHEN IT LIVED: Late Cretaceous (75-81 MYA)

FOUND IN: Mongolia

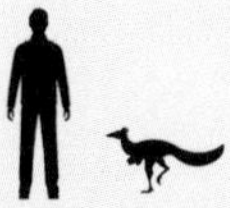

A
B
C
D
E
F
G
H
I
J
K
L
M
N
O
P
Q
R
S
T
U
V
W
X
Y
Z

SILVISAURUS

(sil-vi-sore-us) **FOREST LIZARD**

Silvisaurus is so-named because it was believed to have lived in an area of dense forest in what is now Kansas, USA. This makes sense because *Silvisaurus* was a strict herbivore. It probably fed upon the conifers and ferns that grew during the Late Cretaceous Period, as well as flowering plants. Some scientists have even suggested that dinosaurs like *Silvisaurus* may have helped spread the first flowering plants around the world by eating their fruit and scattering their seeds.

LENGTH: 13 ft

DIET: Herbivorous

WHEN IT LIVED: Late Cretaceous (121-112 MYA)

FOUND IN: USA

FIGURE 146: *Silvisaurus*

A
B
C
D
E
F
G
H
I
J
K
L
M
N
O
P
Q
R
S
T
U
V
W
X
Y
Z

SINOCALLIOPTERYX

(sie-no-kall-ee-op-ter-iks)

CHINESE BEAUTIFUL FEATHER

Sinocalliopteryx was a small, agile hunter in the forests of Early Cretaceous Asia. It was probably covered with feathers, which would have kept it warm and may have also been used to display to others of its kind. However, *Sinocalliopteryx* could not fly, as it did not have wings. Its tail was very long— almost as long as the rest of its body.

LENGTH: 8 ft

DIET: Carnivorous

WHEN IT LIVED: Early Cretaceous (125 MYA)

FOUND IN: People's Republic of China

SINORNITHOSAURUS

(sine-or-nith-oh-sore-us) **CHINESE BIRD LIZARD**

LENGTH: 6.5 ft

DIET: Carnivorous

WHEN IT LIVED: Early Cretaceous (122-120 MYA)

FOUND IN: People's Republic of China

FIGURE 147: *Sinocalliopteryx*

SINOVENATOR

(sien-oh-vee-nay-tor) **CHINESE HUNTER**

Sinovenator was a small predator—probably no bigger than a chicken today. Just like a chicken, it would also have been covered with feathers, because it belonged to a group of dinosaurs that would eventually give rise to modern birds. It was a fast runner and probably lived in areas of woodland.

LENGTH: 3 ft

DIET: Carnivorous

WHEN IT LIVED: Early Cretaceous (127-121 MYA)

FOUND IN: People's Republic of China

FIGURE 148: *Sinovenator*

SINRAPTOR

(sien-rap-tor) **CHINESE PLUNDERER**

LENGTH: 25 ft

DIET: Carnivorous

WHEN IT LIVED: Mid Jurassic (169-142 MYA)

FOUND IN: People's Republic of China

SONIDOSAURUS

(soh-nid-oh-sore-us) **SONID (AREA)**

LENGTH: 30 ft

DIET: Herbivorous

WHEN IT LIVED: Late Cretaceous (89-65 MYA)

FOUND IN: People's Republic of China

SPINOPS

(SPINE-ops) **SPINE FACE**

LENGTH: 20 ft

DIET: Herbivorous

WHEN IT LIVED: Late Cretaceous (76 MYA)

FOUND IN: Canada

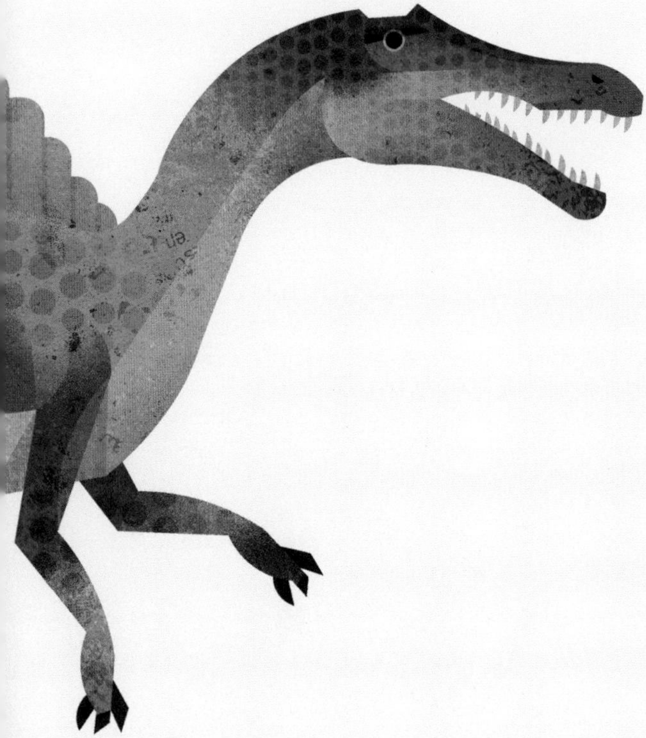

SPINOSAURUS

(SPINE-oh-SORE-us) **THORN LIZARD**

The original fossil of *Spinosaurus* was sadly lost during World War II. From the sketches made by the first people to find it, it seemed to have a big sail along its back and a long, crocodile-like snout. More recent finds suggest its arms were about the same length as its legs, and so it might have walked on four legs instead of two—unlike other meat-eating dinosaurs. It might also have been able to swim, to catch prey in the water. However, some scientists think that the arms and legs of the new fossils did not actually belong to the same creature.

LENGTH: 60 ft

DIET: Carnivorous

WHEN IT LIVED: Late Cretaceous (95-70 MYA)

FOUND IN: Egypt and Morocco

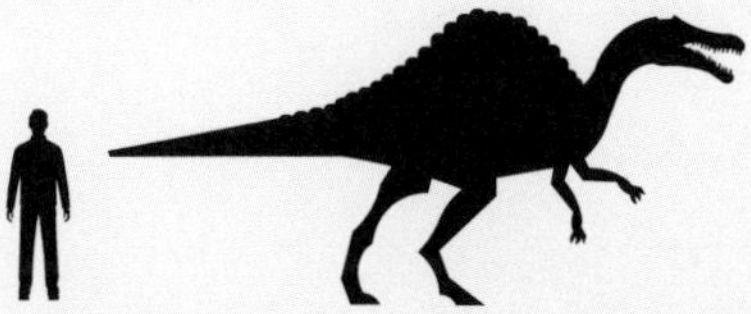

FIGURE 149: *Spinosaurus*

STAURIKOSAURUS

(stor-ik-oh-sore-us) **SOUTHERN CROSS LIZARD**

Staurikosaurus was a medium-sized carnivore which would have hunted smaller dinosaurs in the earliest stage of the dinosaurs' time on Earth. It belonged to a group called the herrerasaurids, which some scientists think were not dinosaurs at all, but close relatives of the early dinosaurs. Others think they are the ancestors of all the meat-eating dinosaurs that were to come later.

LENGTH: 6.5 m

DIET: Carnivorous

WHEN IT LIVED: Late Triassic (227-221 MYA)

FOUND IN: Brazil

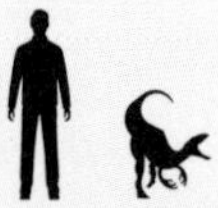

STEGOCERAS

(ste-GOS-er-as) **HORNY ROOF**

LENGTH: 8 ft

DIET: Herbivorous

WHEN IT LIVED: Late Cretaceous (76-74 MYA)

FOUND IN: Canada and USA

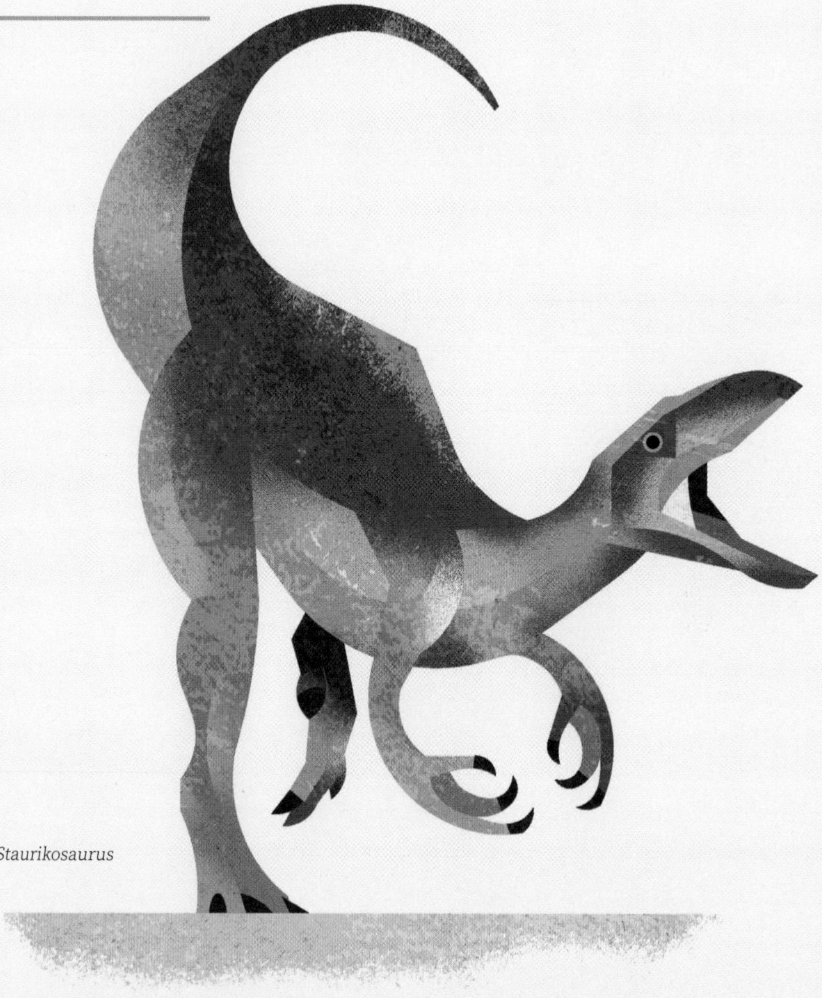

FIGURE 150: *Staurikosaurus*

STEGOSAURUS

(STEG-oh-SORE-us) **ROOF LIZARD**

A large, slow-moving plant-eater, *Stegosaurus* would have defended itself from predators like *Allosaurus* (page 14) and *Ceratosaurus* (page 41) with its powerful spiked tail. It also had bony plates that might have been used to warn off predators, or allowed members of the same species to recognize one another. It is possible they might also have been used to control its body temperature. Compared with the rest of its body, *Stegosaurus* had a small head, and its brain was only about the size of a plum.

LENGTH: 30 ft

DIET: Herbivorous

WHEN IT LIVED: Late Jurassic (156-144 MYA)

FOUND IN: USA

FIGURE 151: *Stegosaurus*

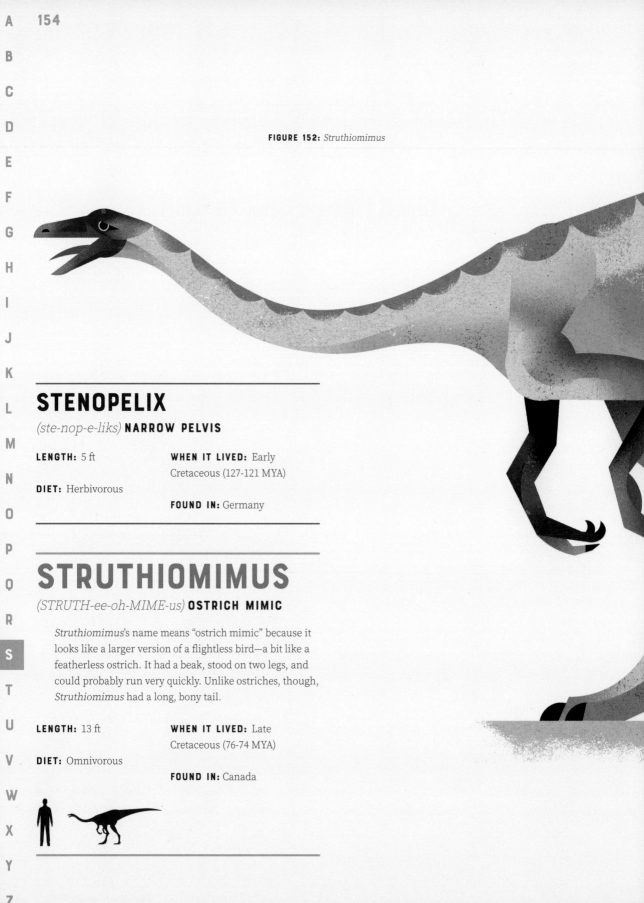

A
B
C
D
E
F
G
H
I
J
K
L
M
N
O
P
Q
R
S
T
U
V
W
X
Y
Z

FIGURE 152: *Struthiomimus*

STENOPELIX

(ste-nop-e-liks) **NARROW PELVIS**

LENGTH: 5 ft

DIET: Herbivorous

WHEN IT LIVED: Early Cretaceous (127-121 MYA)

FOUND IN: Germany

STRUTHIOMIMUS

(STRUTH-ee-oh-MIME-us) **OSTRICH MIMIC**

Struthiomimus's name means "ostrich mimic" because it looks like a larger version of a flightless bird—a bit like a featherless ostrich. It had a beak, stood on two legs, and could probably run very quickly. Unlike ostriches, though, *Struthiomimus* had a long, bony tail.

LENGTH: 13 ft

DIET: Omnivorous

WHEN IT LIVED: Late Cretaceous (76-74 MYA)

FOUND IN: Canada

STYGIMOLOCH

(stij-i-mol-ok) **STYX DEMON**

LENGTH: 10 ft

DIET: Herbivorous

WHEN IT LIVED: Late Cretaceous (67-65 MYA)

FOUND IN: USA

FIGURE 153: *Styracosaurus*

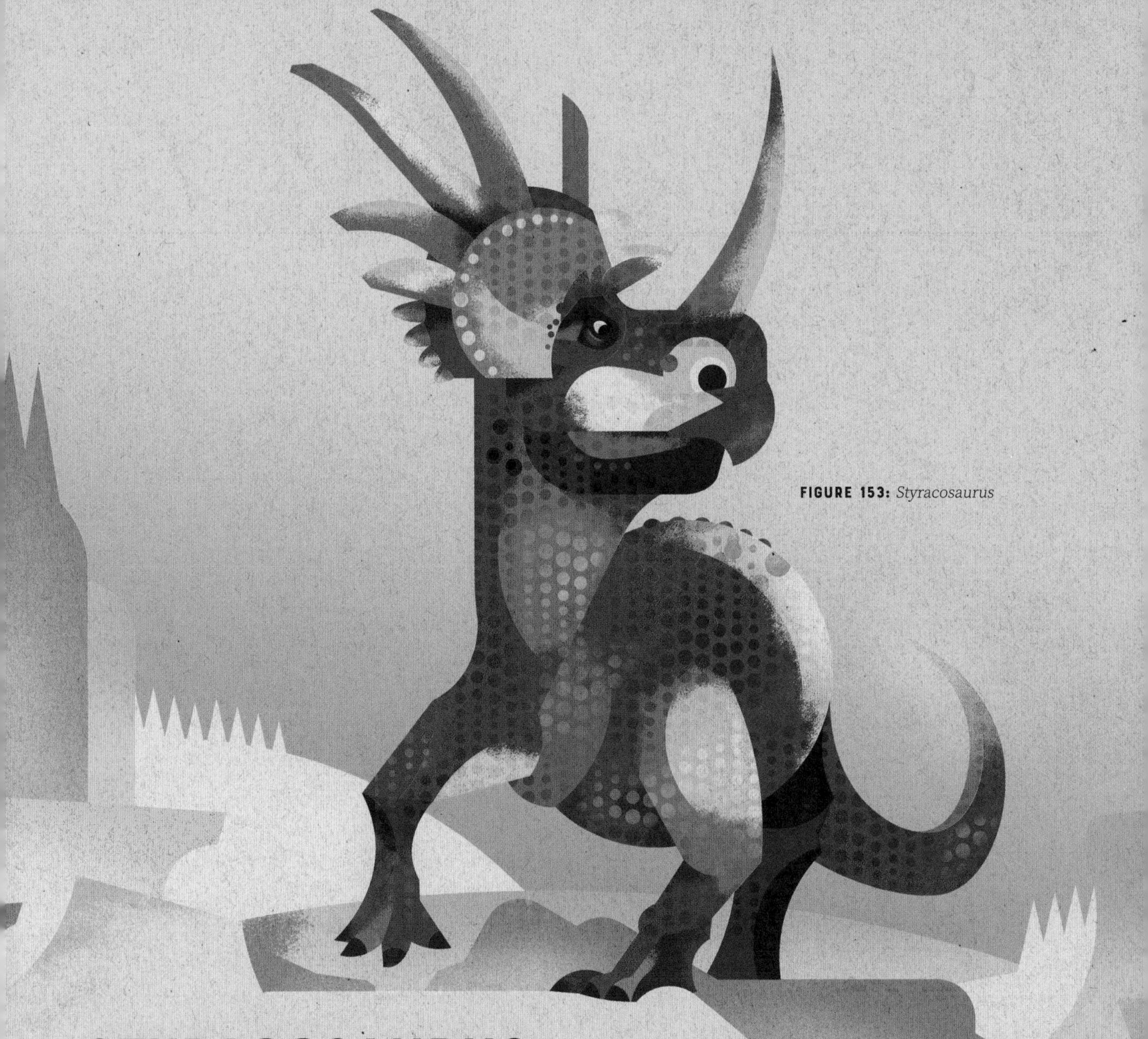

STYRACOSAURUS

(sty-RAK-oh-sore-us) **SPIKED LIZARD**

Styracosaurus was one of the most unique-looking ceratopsians, with a huge row of long spikes that stood out around the rim of its large neck frill and a massive horn on its nose. It ate plants, walked on four legs, and was almost certainly very slow. The spikes may have been for defense against predators, because it probably could not outrun them.

LENGTH: 18 ft

DIET: Herbivorous

WHEN IT LIVED: Late Cretaceous (76-70 MYA)

FOUND IN: Canada and USA

SUCHOMIMUS

(sook-o-mime-us) **CROCODILE MIMIC**

This dinosaur was very similar to *Spinosaurus* (page 151) and *Baryonyx* (page 31). Its snout was long and thin and looked more like the snout of a crocodile than that of other meat-eating dinosaurs. It is believed that it used this snout to hunt for large fish in shallow water. It had lots of long, thin teeth lining its mouth and a rounded lower jaw, which would have been well-suited to catching slippery fish.

LENGTH: 36 ft

DIET: Carnivorous

WHEN IT LIVED: Early Cretaceous (121-112 MYA)

FOUND IN: Niger

FIGURE 154: *Suchomimus*

SUPERSAURUS

(sue-per-sore-us) **SUPER LIZARD**

Scientists have found enough fossil material from this dinosaur to know that it must have been one of the most enormous animals to have ever walked on land. Some estimates of its size suggest it weighed about 44 tons, and it was about 131 feet in length from head to tail. It would have had a similar build to *Apatosaurus* (page 20) but with one of the longest-known necks of all the sauropods.

LENGTH: 115-148 ft

DIET: Herbivorous

WHEN IT LIVED: Early Cretaceous (154-142 MYA)

FOUND IN: USA

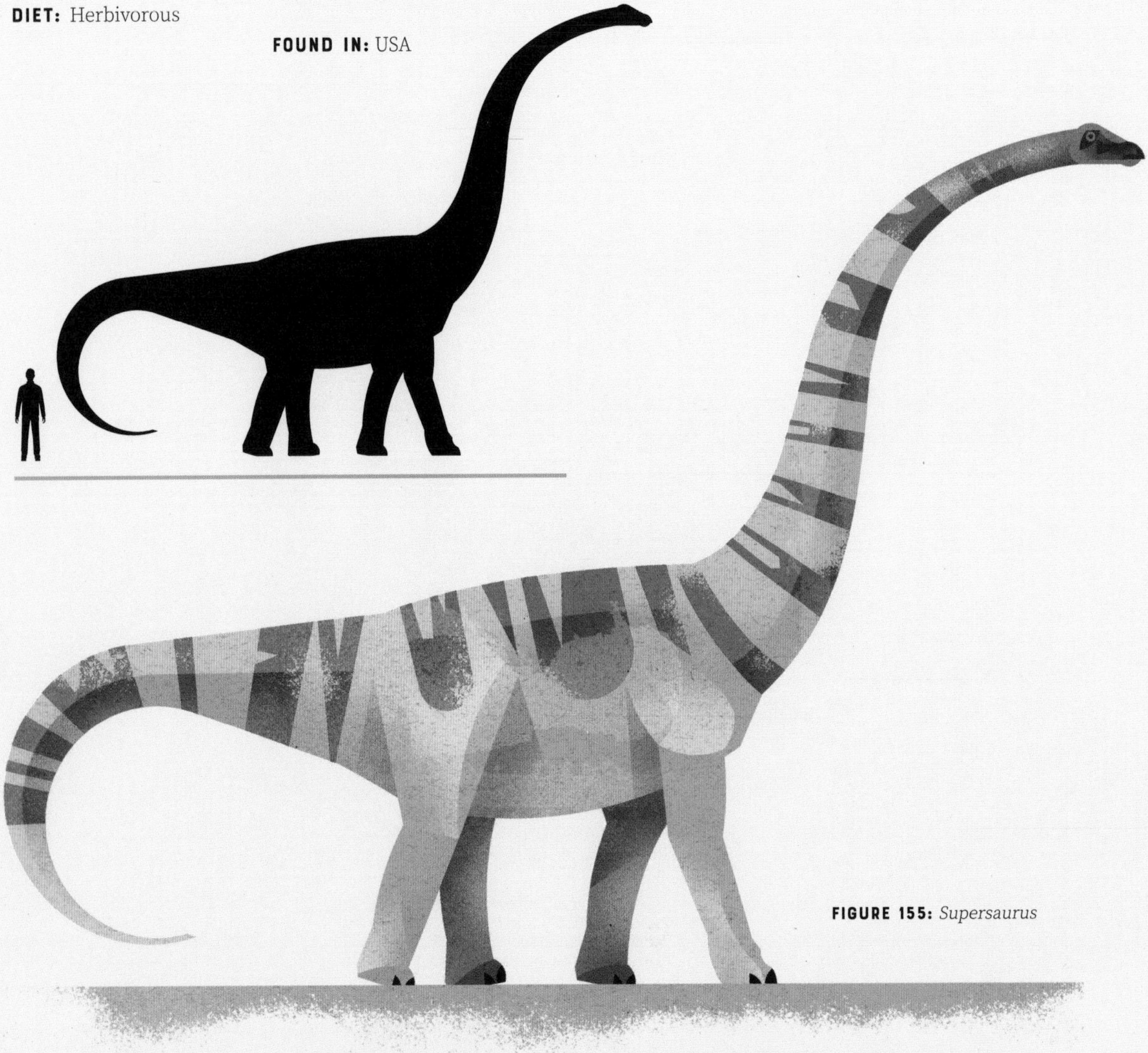

SYNTARSUS

(sin-tar-sus) **FUSED TARSUS**

LENGTH: 2.15m

DIET: Carnivorous

WHEN IT LIVED: Late Triassic (205-190 MYA)

FOUND IN: South Africa, USA and Zimbabwe

FIGURE 155: *Supersaurus*

T - Z

T

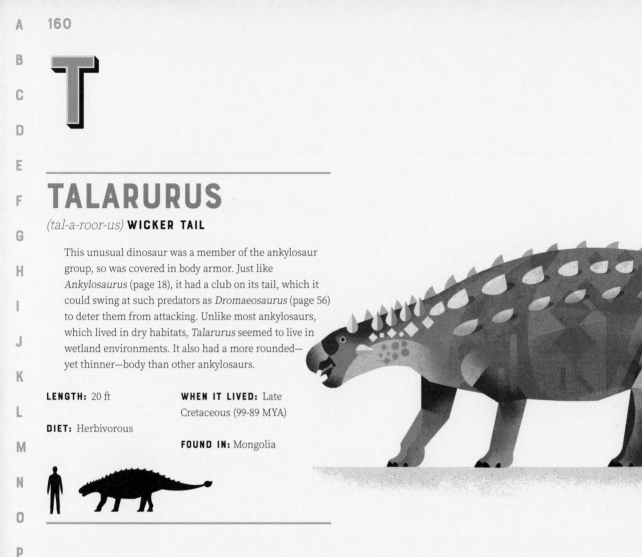

TALARURUS

(tal-a-roor-us) **WICKER TAIL**

This unusual dinosaur was a member of the ankylosaur group, so was covered in body armor. Just like *Ankylosaurus* (page 18), it had a club on its tail, which it could swing at such predators as *Dromaeosaurus* (page 56) to deter them from attacking. Unlike most ankylosaurs, which lived in dry habitats, *Talarurus* seemed to live in wetland environments. It also had a more rounded— yet thinner—body than other ankylosaurs.

LENGTH: 20 ft

DIET: Herbivorous

WHEN IT LIVED: Late Cretaceous (99-89 MYA)

FOUND IN: Mongolia

TANIUS

(tahn-ee-us) **OF TAN [SCIENTIST H.C. TAN]**

LENGTH: 23 ft

DIET: Herbivorous

WHEN IT LIVED: Late Cretaceous (89-65 MYA)

FOUND IN: People's Republic of China

TARBOSAURUS

(TAR-bow-SORE-us) **ALARMING LIZARD**

LENGTH: 32 ft

DIET: Carnivorous

WHEN IT LIVED: Late Cretaceous (74-70 MYA)

FOUND IN: People's Republic of China, Mongolia

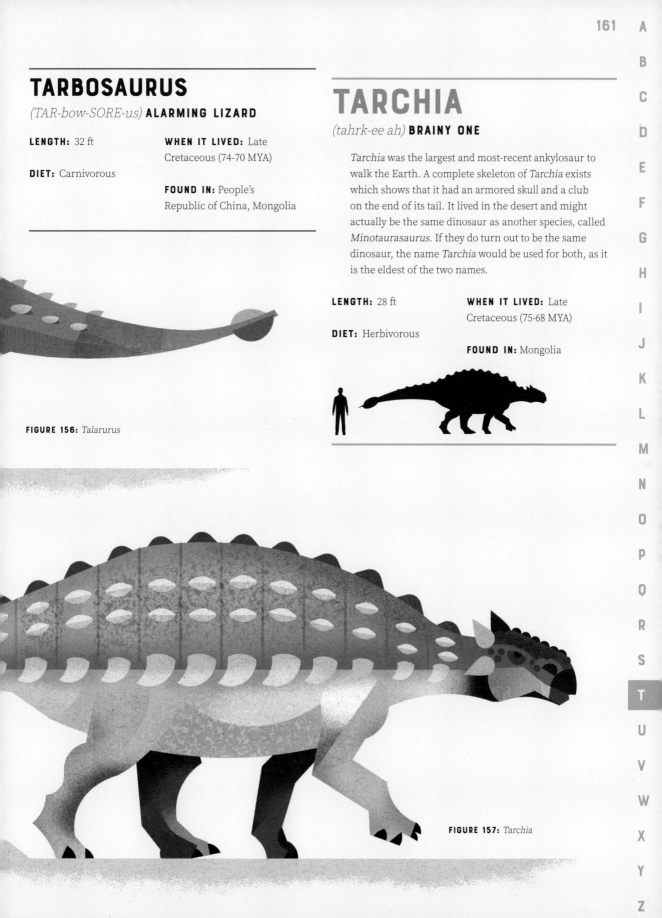

FIGURE 156: *Talarurus*

TARCHIA

(tahrk-ee ah) **BRAINY ONE**

Tarchia was the largest and most-recent ankylosaur to walk the Earth. A complete skeleton of *Tarchia* exists which shows that it had an armored skull and a club on the end of its tail. It lived in the desert and might actually be the same dinosaur as another species, called *Minotaurasaurus*. If they do turn out to be the same dinosaur, the name *Tarchia* would be used for both, as it is the eldest of the two names.

LENGTH: 28 ft

DIET: Herbivorous

WHEN IT LIVED: Late Cretaceous (75-68 MYA)

FOUND IN: Mongolia

FIGURE 157: *Tarchia*

A B C D E F G H I J K L M N O P Q R S T U V W X Y Z

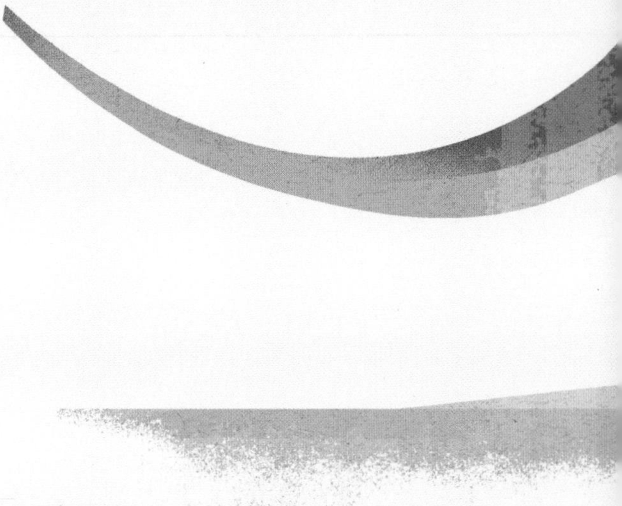

TELMATOSAURUS

(tel-ma-toh-sore-us) **SWAMP LIZARD**

LENGTH: 16 ft

DIET: Herbivorous

WHEN IT LIVED: Late Cretaceous (84-65 MYA)

FOUND IN: Spain, France, Romania

TENONTOSAURUS

(ten-ON-toe-sore-us) **SINEW LIZARD**

Tenontosaurus was a small- to medium-sized herbivore that stood at about the same height as a donkey. It would have been able to run on two legs if it needed to, or to rear up on its hind legs to reach higher foliage, but it more than likely used all four legs day-to-day. Its most striking feature was its tail, which made up more than half of its entire overall length.

LENGTH: 23 ft

DIET: Herbivorous

WHEN IT LIVED: Early Cretaceous (120-110 MYA)

FOUND IN: Canada and USA

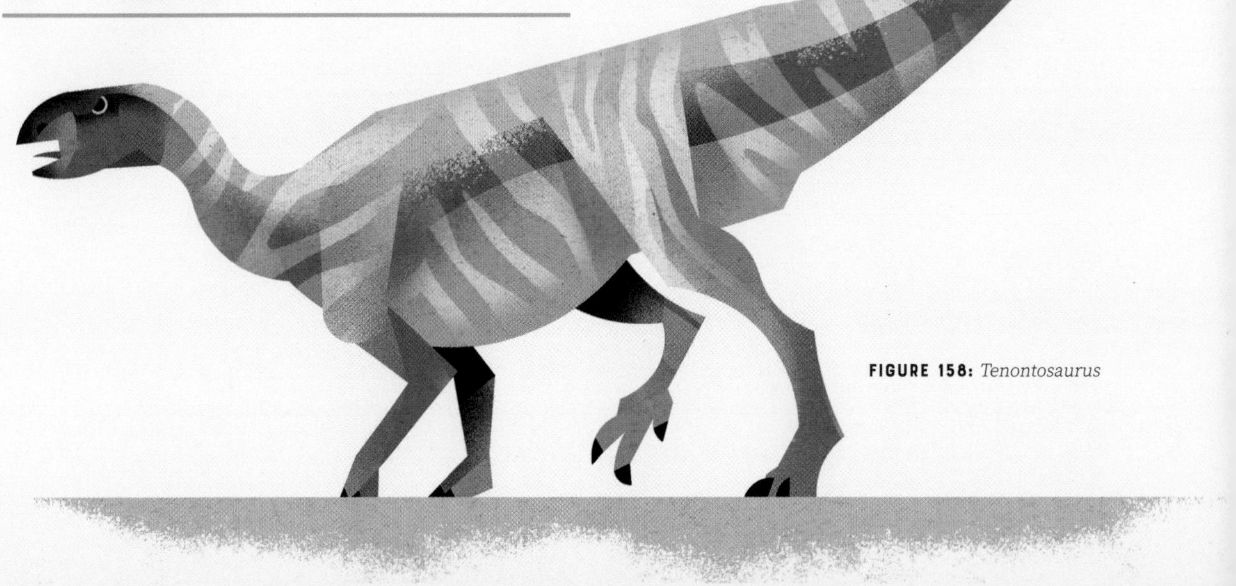

FIGURE 158: *Tenontosaurus*

FIGURE 159: *Thecodontosaurus*

THECODONTOSAURUS

(theek-o-don-toh-sore-us) **SOCKET-TOOTHED LIZARD**

Thecodontosaurus was a small dinosaur that was not much bigger than an average dog today. However, its descendants eventually evolved to become some of the most enormous sauropods on the planet—like *Diplodocus* (page 55) and *Brachiosaurus* (page 33). Although many of its close relatives ate both meat and plant material, *Thecodontosaurus* had leaf-shaped teeth that suggest it was a herbivore.

LENGTH: Up to 8 ft

DIET: Herbivorous

WHEN IT LIVED: Late Triassic (227-205 MYA)

FOUND IN: England

THERIZINOSAURUS

(THER-ih-zine-oh-SORE-us) **SCYTHE LIZARD**

LENGTH: 32 ft

DIET: Unknown

WHEN IT LIVED: Late Cretaceous (85-70 MYA)

FOUND IN: Mongolia

A B C D E F G H I J K L M N O P Q R S T U V W X Y Z

THESCELOSAURUS

(thes-kel-oh-SORE-us) **WONDERFUL LIZARD**

LENGTH: 11 ft

DIET: Herbivorous

WHEN IT LIVED: Late Cretaceous (76-67 MYA)

FOUND IN: Canada and USA

TOROSAURUS

(tor-oh-SORE-us) **BULL LIZARD**

LENGTH: 25 ft

DIET: Herbivorous

WHEN IT LIVED: Late Cretaceous (70-65 MYA)

FOUND IN: Canada and USA

FIGURE 160: *Torvosaurus*

TORVOSAURUS

(TOR-voh-SORE-us) **SAVAGE LIZARD**

Torvosaurus was a large predator. Its jaws were filled with lots of very long and sharp teeth that were curved backward and serrated, like a steak knife, so that they could tear through meat. It also had short but powerful arms. Its prey probably included plated dinosaurs such as *Stegosaurus* (page 153) and the young of sauropods like *Diplodocus* (page 55).

LENGTH: 32 ft

DIET: Carnivorous

WHEN IT LIVED: Late Jurassic (155-144 MYA)

FOUND IN: USA

TRICERATOPS

(try-SERRA-tops) **THREE-HORNED FACE**

With its three horns, a parrot-like beak, and a huge neck frill, the *Triceratops* skull is one of the most striking of any land animal to ever exist. This dinosaur's horns could have been used to fend off attacks from *Tyrannosaurus* (page 169), because a *Triceratops* fossil collected in 1997 shows a horn that was bitten off, with bite marks matching those of *Tyrannosaurus*. It also shows that the horn healed after being bitten, so at least some *Triceratops* survived the attacks. The Triceratops neck frill might have helped to protect its neck, but some specimens show *Tyrannosaurus* bite marks on the frill, so it was not always enough. Other puncture marks on their frills show that male *Triceratops* also used their horns to fight each other—probably to impress females.

LENGTH: 30 ft

DIET: Herbivorous

WHEN IT LIVED: Late Cretaceous (67-65 MYA)

FOUND IN: USA

FIGURE 161: *Triceratops*

A B C D E F G H I J K L M N O P Q R S T U V W X Y Z

TROODON

(TROH-oh-don)

WOUNDING TOOTH

Troodon was a small carnivore that resembled a big version of a modern bird. It laid eggs in nests in the same way as birds do today, and would have been just as smart—with some of the biggest brains of any dinosaur group. It had many razor-sharp teeth for eating meat, which were covered in sharp serrations. Its back legs were very long, suggesting that it could run very quickly.

LENGTH: 6.5 ft

DIET: Carnivorous

WHEN IT LIVED: Late Cretaceous (74-65 MYA)

FOUND IN: USA

TSAGANTEGIA

(tsah-gahn-tay-gee-a) **TSAGAN TEG**

LENGTH: 13-16 ft

DIET: Herbivorous

WHEN IT LIVED: Late Cretaceous (99-84 MYA)

FOUND IN: Mongolia

FIGURE 162: *Troodon*

TSINTAOSAURUS

(ching-dow-sore-us) **QINGDAO LIZARD**

Unlike other hadrosaurs, this dinosaur had a very long spike pointing out from its skull. Other hadrosaurs like *Parasaurolophus* (page 122) had crests on their heads, so *Tsintaosaurus's* spike is quite unusual. Scientists do not know what this spike was for. Perhaps it was used by *Tsintaosaurus* for identifying others of its kind, or to attract a mate. Some have suggested that only the males of the species would have had the spike, but others disagree—and only the discovery of more fossils will hold the answer.

LENGTH: 40-60 ft

DIET: Herbivorous

WHEN IT LIVED: Late Cretaceous (84-71 MYA)

FOUND IN: People's Republic of China

FIGURE 163: *Tsintaosaurus*

TUOJIANGOSAURUS

(too-YANG-oh-sore-us) **TUO RIVER LIZARD**

LENGTH: 23 ft

DIET: Herbivorous

WHEN IT LIVED: Late Jurassic (157-154 MYA)

FOUND IN: People's Republic of China

A
B
C
D
E
F
G
H
I
J
K
L
M
N
O
P
Q
R
S
T
U
V
W
X
Y
Z

TYLOCEPHALE

(tie-loh-keff-ah-lee) **SWELLING HEAD**

Tylocephale was a pachycephalosaur, so it had a thick, ridged skull. Not much fossil material of this dinosaur exists, but by looking at its closest relatives, we can tell that it walked on two legs and ate plants. It also had a dome on its head, possibly used for fighting with other dinosaurs. It is believed to have been the tallest head dome of any of the pachycephalosaurs.

LENGTH: 4.5 ft

DIET: Herbivorous

WHEN IT LIVED: Late Cretaceous (75-72 MYA)

FOUND IN: Mongolia

FIGURE 164: *Tylocephale*

FIGURE 165: *Tyrannosaurus*

TYRANNOSAURUS

(tie-RAN-oh-sore-us) **TYRANT LIZARD**

Tyrannosaurus lives up to its reputation as one of the most fearsome meat-eaters of all time. Its powerful jaw had 60 teeth, each one about 8 inches long, and its bite was about three times more powerful than a lion's. Bite marks found on *Triceratops* (page 165) fossils show that *Tyrannosaurus* could crunch through bone, and fossilized dung contained the bones of its prey. It could use its good sense of smell to hunt and locate dead bodies to scavenge. It would have been able to scare off any other scavengers, so it did not have to share a kill. We do not know whether *Tyrannosaurus* hunted alone or in packs, as no groups of skeletons have been found together.

LENGTH: 40 ft

DIET: Carnivorous

WHEN IT LIVED: Late Cretaceous (67-65 MYA)

FOUND IN: Canada and USA

A
B
C
D
E
F
G
H
I
J
K
L
M
N
O
P
Q
R
S
T
U
V
W
X
Y
Z

UDANOCERATOPS

(oo-dahn-oh-serra-tops) **UDAN HORNED FACE**

Udanoceratops was a ceratopsian, but it had hardly any head frill, unlike other ceratopsians. This strange-looking dinosaur had a very deep lower jaw, which suggests that it had powerful muscles for chewing. This would have allowed it to grind up and swallow even the toughest plants for food. It may have also swallowed "gizzard" stones to help digest this material.

FIGURE 166: *Udanoceratops*

LENGTH: 13-16 ft

DIET: Herbivorous

WHEN IT LIVED: Late Cretaceous (81-75 MYA)

FOUND IN: Mongolia

UNENLAGIA

(oon-en-lahg-ee-ah) **HALF BIRD**

LENGTH: 8 ft

DIET: Carnivorous

WHEN IT LIVED: Late Cretaceous (94-86 MYA)

FOUND IN: Argentina

URBACODON

(urb-ah-ko-don) **URBAC TOOTH**

LENGTH: 3 ft

DIET: Carnivorous

WHEN IT LIVED: Late Cretaceous (95 MYA)

FOUND IN: Uzbekistan

UTAHRAPTOR

(YOO-tah-RAP-tor) **UTAH PLUNDERER**

Utahraptor looked similar to *Velociraptor* (page 172), but was much larger. In fact, it was one of the largest members of the raptor family. Like *Velociraptor*, it had good eyesight, sharp teeth, and a razor sharp-claw on each foot for killing its prey. Research has shown that this claw was used for stabbing, not slashing, and may have been particularly useful for wounding the herbivores that it hunted.

LENGTH: 20 ft

DIET: Carnivorous

WHEN IT LIVED: Early Cretaceous (112-100 MYA)

FOUND IN: USA

V

VALDOSAURUS

(val-doh-sore-us) **WEALDEN LIZARD**

LENGTH: 10 ft

DIET: Herbivorous

WHEN IT LIVED: Early Cretaceous (142-121 MYA)

FOUND IN: England, Niger, Romania

FIGURE 167: *Utahraptor*

VELOCIRAPTOR

(vel-OSS-ee-rap-tor) **QUICK PLUNDERER**

In the Jurassic Park films, the raptor *Velociraptor* was re-created at twice its actual size and closely modeled on *Deinonychus* (page 52). In reality, *Velociraptor* was only the size of a turkey and is now thought to have had a fine feather-like covering. Its arms were too short to allow it to fly or glide, but it might have kept its feathers to balance its body temperature or help keep its eggs warm when nesting. *Velociraptor* had three curved claws on its hands and a sickle-shaped talon on each foot, which it might have used as hooks to prevent prey from escaping.

LENGTH: 6 ft

DIET: Carnivorous

WHEN IT LIVED: Late Cretaceous (84-80 MYA)

FOUND IN: Mongolia

FIGURE 168: *Velociraptor*

VULCANODON

(vul-kan-oh-don) **VOLCANO TOOTH**

Found on a small island in the middle of a lake, *Vulcanodon* was a prosauropod, and thought to have been one of the links between two-legged, early dinosaurs like *Massospondylus* (page 102) and the larger, four-legged sauropods like *Brachiosaurus* (page 33). Its name means "volcano tooth" because one fossil was found along with teeth between two layers of volcanic rock, but the teeth later turned out to belong to a theropod that had been eating the *Vulcanodon's* body.

LENGTH: 21 ft

DIET: Herbivorous

WHEN IT LIVED: Early Jurassic (200-190 MYA)

FOUND IN: Zimbabwe

WINTONOTITAN

(wint-o-no-ti-tan) **WINTON (TOWN) TITAN**

LENGTH: About 50-53 ft

DIET: Herbivorous

WHEN IT LIVED: Early Cretaceous (112-100 MYA)

FOUND IN: Australia

WUERHOSAURUS

(woo-uhr-huh-sore-us) **WUERHO LIZARD**

LENGTH: 23-26 ft

DIET: Herbivorous

WHEN IT LIVED: Early Cretaceous (137-99 MYA)

FOUND IN: People's Republic of China

FIGURE 169: *Vulcanodon*

XENOPOSEIDON

(ZEEN-no-puh-SYE-d'n) **STRANGE POSEIDON**

LENGTH: 32 ft

DIET: Herbivorous

WHEN IT LIVED: Early Cretaceous (140 MYA)

FOUND IN: England

XENOTARSOSAURUS

(ZEEN-o-TAR-so-SORE-us)
STRANGE ANKLE LIZARD

LENGTH: About 20 ft

DIET: Carnivorous

WHEN IT LIVED: Late Cretaceous (100-90 MYA)

FOUND IN: Argentina

FIGURE 170: *Xiaotingia*

XIAOSAURUS

(shyow-SORE-us) **DAWN LIZARD**

LENGTH: 3 ft

DIET: Herbivorous

WHEN IT LIVED: Middle Jurassic (169-163 MYA)

FOUND IN: People's Republic of China

XIAOTINGIA

(shyow-TING-gee-uh) **(NAMED AFTER ZHENG XIAOTING, FOUNDER OF THE SHANDONGTIANYU MUSEUM)**

Xiaotingia was a birdlike dinosaur, with feathers covering the body and longer plumes on the arms, legs and tail, giving it four wings. Like *Microraptor* (page 106), these might have allowed it to glide or fly through the air. But it also had teeth and a long, bony tail, so it looked a bit like *Archaeopteryx* (page 22). Its teeth would have been very effective for preying on hard-shelled insects or crunching through plant material.

LENGTH: About 1.5 ft

DIET: Carnivorous

WHEN IT LIVED: Late Jurassic (160 MYA)

FOUND IN: People's Republic of China

Y

YANDUSAURUS

(yen-doo-sore-us) **YANDU LIZARD**

At about 13 feet in length from head to tail, *Yandusaurus* was one of the smaller herbivores of its time. Like the later dinosaur *Hypsilophodon* (page 82), it ran on two legs and saved its hands for grasping things. The fossils of *Yandusaurus* were discovered by accident in 1973 when Chinese construction workers started digging up earth, so some of the first *Yandusaurus* fossil was destroyed.

LENGTH: About 13 ft

DIET: Herbivorous

WHEN IT LIVED: Mid Jurassic (169-159 MYA)

FOUND IN: People's Republic of China

FIGURE 171: *Yandusaurus*

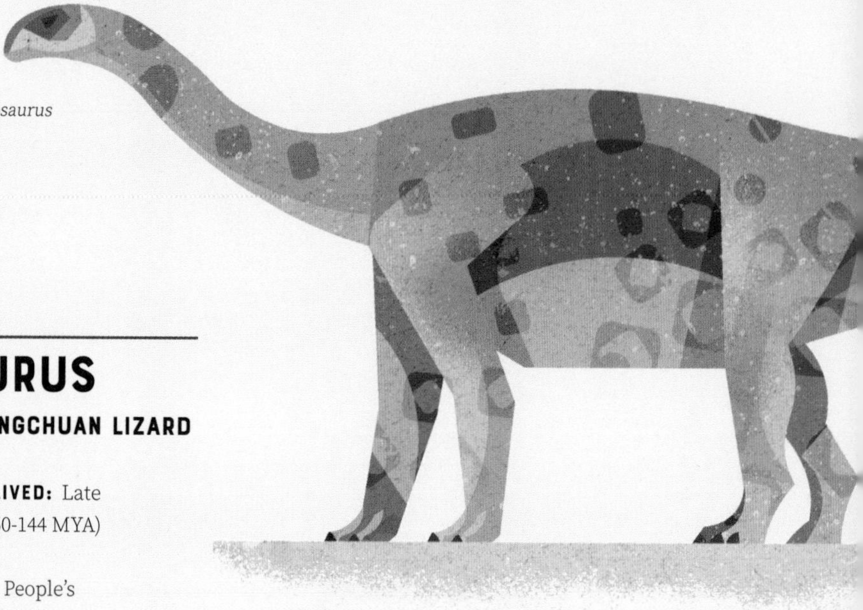

FIGURE 172: *Yimenosaurus*

YANGCHUANOSAURUS

(yang-choo-AHN-oh-SORE-us) **YANGCHUAN LIZARD**

LENGTH: 32 ft

DIET: Carnivorous

WHEN IT LIVED: Late Jurassic (160-144 MYA)

FOUND IN: People's Republic of China

YIMENOSAURUS

(yee-muhn-oh-sore-us) **YIMEN LIZARD**

Yimenosaurus was an early form of a sauropod and was most similar to European sauropods like *Plateosaurus* (page 127). It was a chunky dinosaur with wide feet. As these early sauropods evolved, their bodies grew bigger and bigger, but they still walked on just two legs. It was another 10 million years before sauropods would abandon walking on two legs altogether to start walking on all four legs.

LENGTH: 30 ft

DIET: Herbivorous

WHEN IT LIVED: Early Jurassic (195-190 MYA)

FOUND IN: People's Republic of China

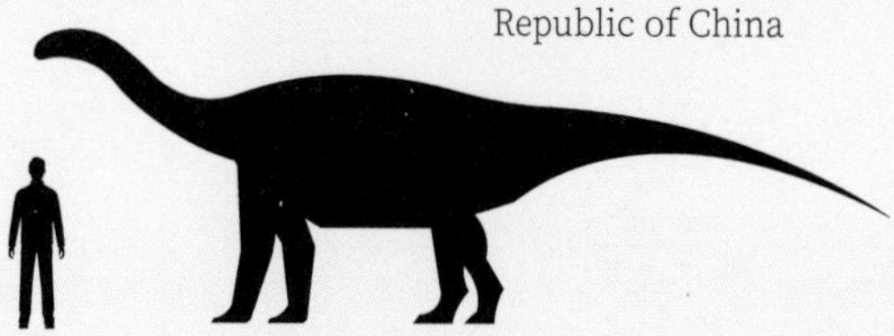

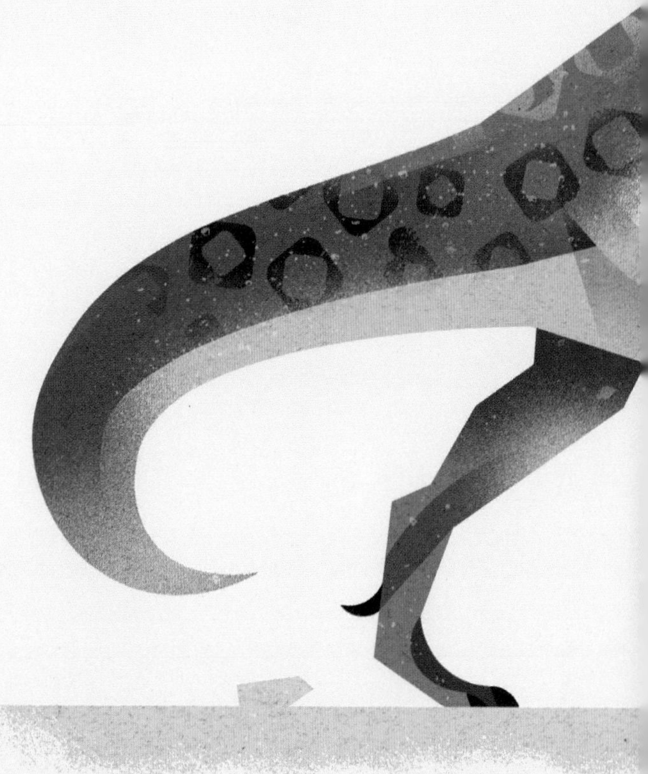

YINGSHANOSAURUS

(ying-shan-oh-sore-us) **MOUNT YING LIZARD**

LENGTH: About 16 ft

DIET: Herbivorous

WHEN IT LIVED: Late Jurassic (159-142 MYA)

FOUND IN: People's Republic of China

YINLONG

(yin-long) **HIDDEN DRAGON**

The earliest-known ceratopsian, *Yinlong* was the ancestor of huge herbivores like *Triceratops*, which would evolve by the Late Cretaceous. However, *Yinlong* itself was rather small. It ate mainly plants, but its mixture of sharp and blunt teeth suggests it might have eaten insects, too. It also swallowed "gizzard" stones to help mash up plant matter and release more nutrients.

LENGTH: 4 ft

DIET: Herbivorous

WHEN IT LIVED: Mid Jurassic (159-154 MYA)

FOUND IN: People's Republic of China

FIGURE 173: *Yinlong*

YUANMOUSAURUS

(ywahn-moo-sore-us) **YUANMOU (AREA)**

LENGTH: 55 feet

DIET: Herbivorous

WHEN IT LIVED: Mid Jurassic (180-159 MYA)

FOUND IN: People's Republic of China

YUNNANOSAURUS

(yoo-nahn-oh-sore-us) **YUNNAN LIZARD**

The fossils of over 20 individual *Yunnanosaurus* have been found. It was an early prosauropod, so it was part of the group of dinosaurs that would eventually give rise to the enormous *Diplodocus* (page 55). It ate plants and, although it mainly walked on four legs, it was also able to rear up on its hind legs to reach higher foliage.

LENGTH: 23 ft

DIET: Omnivorous

WHEN IT LIVED: Early Jurassic (205-190 MYA)

FOUND IN: People's Republic of China

YUTYRANNUS

(yoo-tie-RAN-us) **FEATHERED GIANT**

LENGTH: 30 ft

DIET: Carnivorous

WHEN IT LIVED: Early Cretaceous (125 MYA)

FOUND IN: People's Republic of China

Z

ZALMOXES

(zal-moks-eez) **ZALMOXES (DACIAN DEITY)**

LENGTH: 10 ft

DIET: Herbivorous

WHEN IT LIVED: Late Cretaceous (69 MYA)

FOUND IN: Romania

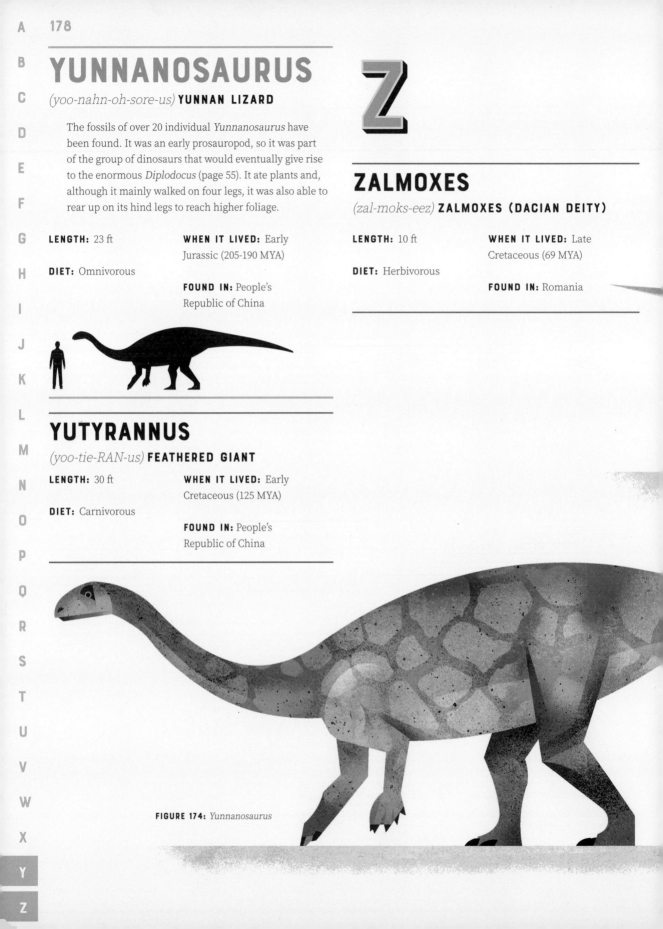

FIGURE 174: *Yunnanosaurus*

ZEPHYROSAURUS

(ZEF-ear-ro-SORE-us) **WEST WIND LIZARD**

Zephyrosaurus was a small dinosaur that lived off the plants that grew in in North America during the Early Cretaceous. It was possibly preyed upon by fearsome dinosaurs like *Deinonychus* (page 52), and would have relied on its speed and agility to stay out of its way. It is also thought to have been able to burrow underground to dig out retreats for escaping from its predators.

FIGURE 175: *Zephyrosaurus*

LENGTH: 6 ft

DIET: Herbivorous

WHEN IT LIVED: Early Cretaceous (120-110 MYA)

FOUND IN: USA

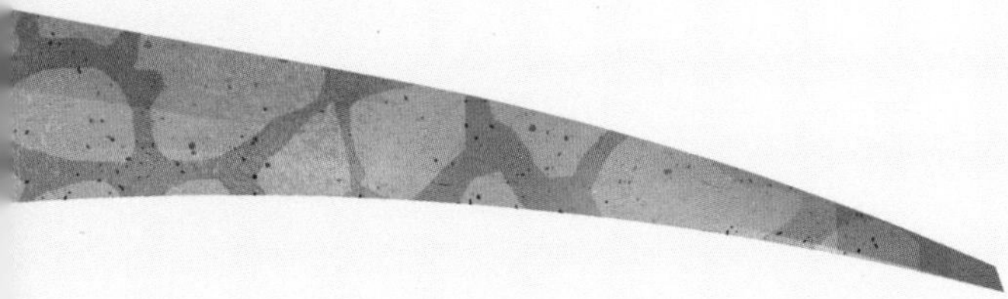

ZHUCHENGTYRANNUS

(zoo-cheng-tie-ran-us) **ZHUCHENG TYRANT**

LENGTH: 36 feet

DIET: Carnivore

WHEN IT LIVED: Late Cretaceous (94-89 MYA)

FOUND IN: People's Republic of China

ZUNICERATOPS

(zoo-nee-serra-tops) **ZUNI (NATIVE AMERICAN PEOPLE) HORNED-FACE**

LENGTH: 10-13 ft

DIET: Herbivorous

WHEN IT LIVED: Late Cretaceous (94-89 MYA)

FOUND IN: USA

Dictionary of Dinosaurs © 2018 Quarto Publishing plc.
Text © 2018 The Trustees of the Natural History Museum, London.
Illustrations © 2018 Dieter Braun. Edited by Dr. Matthew G. Baron.

First Published in 2018 by Wide Eyed Editions, an imprint of The Quarto Group.
100 Cummings Center, Suite 265D, Beverly, MA 01915, USA.
T (978) 282-9590 F (978) 283-2742 **www.Quarto.com**

Published in partnership with the Natural History Museum, London.

A catalogue record for this book is available from the British Library.

ISBN 978-0-7112-9053-2

The illustrations were created digitally
Set in Bourton and Source Serif Pro

Published by Rachel Williams and Jenny Broom
Designed by Nicola Price
Design assistance from Sasha Moxon
Copy edited by Eryl Nash
Project edited by Katy Flint
Production by Catherine Cragg
Cover designed by Lyli Feng

Manufactured in Guangdong, China TT102023

9 8 7 6 5 4 3 2 1